30 YEARS ADVOCATING F

CAROLYN

MW01701725

UNDERSTANDING HOW TO BE AN

ADVOCATE FOR ME!

An Elementary to Secondary Education Guide
For Special Education Services and 504
Parents and Students

Understanding how to be an advocate for me! An Elementary to Secondary Guide for Special Education Services and 504 Parents and Students

Copyright ©2023 by Carolyn Ann Morris
Published by Rock Dimensional Consulting, LLC
ISBN: 979-8-218-31421-7

All rights reserved. No part of this guide may be reproduced or transmitted in any form or by any means, electronic or mechanical, including photocopying or recording the author, except for the inclusion of quotations in a review without written permission from the author.

This guide is for informational purposes. Any similarities and information for special education and 504 services are aligned with the Texas Education Agency and IDEA. The advocate is not responsible for the outcome of any Due Process hearings, suits, or damages based on the information provided.

PRINTED IN THE UNITED STATES OF AMERICA.

Dedications

My daughters Ketra and Nina and my son Marcus (deceased), Grandchildren Keenan, Kennedi, Shambregia, Marcus Jr, Paige, and Prince, Great grandchild Za'Adrianna. To all individuals with disabilities, non-disabled, and individuals who seek change in their lives to be heard and to receive services.

Special Thanks

To my mother, Zelma, and grandmother, Orado, for their commitment and for giving back to the Community. My mother instilled in me the person that I am today—serving the Lord first and giving back extraordinarily, volunteering and standing for fairness and justice for all. These two individuals' strengths have molded me into who I am today.

Credits

Pastor Dr. Denny D. Davis, Saint John, Baptist Church
Grand Prairie, Texas.
"*Stay the course*"

Thank you to my daughters, Dr. Ketra L. Davenport-King and Nina L. Morris-Richardson, for supporting me over the years and understanding the importance of being an advocate for their children and giving back to their communities. My journey started and continues based on my late son Marcus D. Davenport's words, "*Do not stop, Mom, you have made a difference for me and my friends.*"

CAROLYN ANN MORRIS

Carolyn Ann Morris grew up in Dallas, Texas, and has resided in Lancaster, Texas, for 39 years, a suburb of Dallas County. Carolyn Ann Morris has impacted the community, schools, parents, and children by advocating for families and children with disabilities.

She has spent the past 40 years in the trenches and being a voice for the underprivileged and unjust in her local, state, and national educational governance. Mrs. Morris stands for fairness for all people and, more importantly, for the residents of the City of Lancaster. Her fight for justice and change will be forever etched in her community, the State of Texas legislative laws, and Lancaster ISD schools.

Her legacy for her community and civic activism will impact future generations. She and her husband are the parents of three children, Dr. Ketra L. Davenport-King (Pastor Willie King), The Honorable Nina L. Morris-Richardson (Prentiss Richardson), and Marcus D. Davenport (Deceased), along with six grandchildren and two great-grandchildren. She holds a Bachelor of Arts and Science from Dallas Baptist University (DBU) and a Paralegal Degree from El Centro College, and she is a certified mediator.

Community and Civil Leadership

Parent-to-Parent Connection Advocacy Inc. PPCA, a 501(c)3 nonprofit organization in 2002, provides advocacy and support services for parents and students in education with disabilities.

The first African American elected to the Lancaster Independence School District Board of Trustees District 3, in 1995-2010, served as President of the Board of Trustees. She is currently serving in District 6 for the LISD Board of Trustees.

Alumni of the Leadership Texas Association of School Board (LTASB), 2004, alumni of The Best Southwest Leadership, 2009, and alumni of United Way of Dallas Blueprint Leadership Program.

Mediator for Dallas County Family & Civil Court & Texas Department of Insurance (TDI).

Dallas Metro Care Mental Health Advisory Board Member Partners in Policymaking for Texans with Development Disabilities.

Texas Associate School Board; National Caucus of Black Schools; Board Members (NSBA)

National School Board Association; Partners in Policymaking for Texans with Developmental Disabilities.

Mrs. Morris is the founding President of the National Association for the Advancement of Colored People (NAACP) in Lancaster, Texas.

MY WHY?

My mission and passion as an advocate for children with disabilities started with my late son, Marcus D. Davenport. He was the middle child with a whole lot of personality. He loved hard, and he loved his family even harder. As a child, he was a busybody, a late walker, very hyper, and had developmental challenges. As a precaution, we had him tested because of the severity of his hyperactivity. The result showed no signs of mental retardation, autism, cerebral palsy, down syndrome, or any other neurological issues. However, we did discover that he was diagnosed with Attention Deficit Hyperactivity Disorder (ADHD). At that unidentified moment in my life, I became a parent advocate. However, I could not have imagined that over 30 years later, the Parent-to-Parent Connection Advocacy, Inc. would have been instrumental in helping hundreds of K-12 grade kids successfully graduate from high school and become advocates for their disability and education.

My journey has come with many challenges. However, the same determination that I was committed to help my son is the same I uphold today. I have spent three decades developing as an advocate to understand disabilities and how they affect children in their educational environments and lives. It was my goal then, and it is my goal now to be the best advocate I can BE!

As I reflect on why I am an advocate, I am reminded daily that I (1) wanted my son to graduate from high school successfully, and he did; (2) I never wanted him to be placed in District Education Alternative Placement (DEAP), and he was not, (3) not be labeled as a BAD kid with behavioral issues, he was not, and (4) to not placed in the Juvenile Justice Alternate Placement (JJAEP). Be advised that, as a young child, he faced each of these scenarios without regard for his disability due to his impulsivity and behaviors.

My son successfully graduated from Lancaster High School in 1998, and the years of my advocacy for him proved to be a success because, after the final due process findings, the school had failed to give him a free appropriate public education (FAPE) due to improperly following his IEP and BIP in the least restrictive environment. It was found that Lancaster Independent School District did, in fact, fail my son, and the school district was ordered to pay for his first two years in college.

As his parent, it was my responsibility to be his advocate, just like it is essential for all parents and children to advocate for themselves and their education. Every time I advocate for a child, I hear the small, still voice from my son reminding me to keep pushing momma, '*You will change their lives just as you changed mine.*'

This is My Why!
Carolyn Ann Morris, Parent Advocate
Parent-to-Parent Connection Advocacy, Inc.

"For everyone to whom much is given, from him much will be required; and to whom much has been committed, of him they will ask the more." (Luke 12:48) NKJV

CONTENTS

What Is Advocacy? 11
What Is An Advocate? 13
What Is Self-Advocacy? 16
The difference between special education services and a 504 service plan.... 18
    Special Education Services (modifications): 18
    Section 504 Service Plan (accommodations): 19
Understanding the Individualized Education Program (IEP) 22
Understanding the 504 Service Plan 25
Tea Individualized Education Program (IEP) Options And Codes 28
    IEP options and codes 28
    504 service plan option and codes 30
The Differences 33
Six Myths about 504 Service Plans 36

ELEMENTARY K-6

I Have An IEP To Receive Special Education Services, Now What? 41
What is the purpose of my Behavior Intervention Plan (BIP)? 45
What Is In The Behavior Intervention Plan (BIP)? 48
What Do I Need To Know About My Behavior Implementation Plan? 52
    How do I know that I need a BIP or an IEP? 54
    Signs that an elementary student may need an IEP: 54
    Signs that an elementary student may need a BIP (in addition to an IEP): 55
What Question Should I Ask My Child's Teacher About The IEP? 57
What Question Should I Ask My Teacher About A 504 Service Plan? 60

SECONDARY 7-12

I Have An IEP To Receive Special Education Services, Now What? 65
What is the purpose of my Behavior Intervention plan (BIP)? 69

What Is In The Behavior Intervention Plan (BIP)? 72
What Do I Need To Know About My Behavior Intervention Plan? 76
The Signs That A Secondary Student Needs an IEP and/or BIP 78
Signs indicating the need for an IEP (Individualized Education Program): 78
Signs Indicating the Need for a BIP (Behavior Intervention Plan): 79
Examples of Questions to Ask the Secondary Teacher 82
Examples Of Questions to Ask the Secondary Teacher About Needing A 504 Service Plan 86
Five Ways to Help K–12 Students Advocate for Themselves 90

APPENDIX

Index to the Terms and Meaning 95
Free Appropriate Public Education (FAPE) at a glance chart 118
Timeline | Child-Centered Special Education Process 120
Student handouts and worksheets
Appendix 1 121
Appendix 2 122
Appendix 3 123
Appendix 4 124
Appendix 5 125
Appendix 6 126
Parent-to-Parent Connection Advocacy, Inc., contact information 127
Bibliography 129

WHAT IS ADVOCACY?

Advocacy refers to supporting, promoting, or speaking out on behalf of a particular cause, issue, group, or individual to bring about social, political, or policy change. Advocacy can take various forms and can be done by individuals, organizations, or communities. It typically involves raising awareness, mobilizing support, and using various strategies to influence decision-makers, public opinion, or policies favoring the cause or group being advocated for.

Key elements of advocacy include:

1. **Awareness and Education:** Advocates often start by raising awareness about an issue or cause. This may involve providing information, statistics, and facts to educate the public and decision-makers about the importance and relevance of the issue.

2. **Building Support:** Advocates work to build a base of support among the public, stakeholders, and influencers who share their goals and values. This support can be critical in gaining momentum and influencing change.

3. **Lobbying and Policy Change:** Advocacy frequently includes efforts to influence government policies and decisions. This can involve lobbying, contacting elected officials, and advocating for specific legislative or regulatory changes.

4. **Public Relations and Media:** Advocates often use media and public relations strategies to reach a broader audience and generate media coverage. This can help bring attention to the issue and create a sense of urgency.

5. **Community Organizing:** Grassroots advocacy involves mobilizing communities and individuals at the local level to advocate for change collectively. This can be a powerful way to build momentum and influence decision-makers.

6. **Legal Action:** In some cases, advocacy may involve legal action, such as filing lawsuits to challenge policies or practices perceived as unjust or harmful.

7. **Collaboration:** Advocacy efforts often involve collaborating with like-minded organizations, coalitions, or individuals to amplify their impact and share resources and expertise.

8. **Peaceful Protest and Activism:** Advocacy can include peaceful protests, demonstrations, and other forms of activism to draw attention to an issue and pressure decision-makers.

9. **Online Advocacy:** In the digital age, online platforms and social media have become powerful tools for advocacy, allowing advocates to reach a global audience and mobilize support quickly.

Advocacy can address a wide range of issues, including human rights, social justice, environmental protection, healthcare reform, education policy, and many others. It plays a crucial role in shaping public discourse, influencing policy decisions, and promoting positive social change.

WHAT IS AN ADVOCATE?

An advocate is a person who actively supports, promotes, or speaks on behalf of a particular cause, issue, group, or individual. Advocates work to raise awareness, generate support, and influence decision-makers or public opinion in favor of the cause or group they represent. They play a crucial role in bringing about social, political, or policy change by using their voice, expertise, and influence to advance their objectives.

Advocates can take many forms and operate at various levels, from grassroots activists to professionals working for advocacy organizations or within government institutions. Some common types of advocates include:

1. **Individual Advocates:** These are passionate about a specific cause or issue and take it upon themselves to raise awareness, educate others, and advocate for change. They may do this through social media, public speaking, community organizing, or other means.

2. **Organizational Advocates:** Advocacy organizations, such as non-governmental organizations (NGOs), nonprofits, and advocacy groups, employ staff or volunteers dedicated to advocating for specific causes or issues. These organizations often have a structured approach to advocacy and may engage in lobbying, public campaigns, and policy research.

3. **Legal Advocates:** Lawyers and legal professionals often serve as advocates for their clients in legal matters. They represent and argue on behalf of their clients' interests in court, during negotiations, or in legal proceedings.

4. **Patient Advocates:** In healthcare, advocates work to ensure patients receive the best possible care and support. They may assist patients in navigating the healthcare system, understanding their rights, and advocating for their medical needs.

5. **Environmental Advocates:** Advocates for environmental causes work to protect and preserve the natural environment. They may campaign for conservation, lobby for environmental policies, and raise awareness about environmental issues.

6. **Human Rights Advocates:** Human rights advocates work to protect and promote human rights and civil liberties. They may focus on issues such as freedom of speech, gender equality, racial justice, and refugee rights.

7. **Child Advocates:** These advocates focus on the well-being and rights of children. They may work in child welfare agencies, nonprofits, or legal settings to ensure that children are protected and have access to education, healthcare, and a safe environment.

8. **Disability Advocates:** Advocates for individuals with disabilities work to promote inclusivity, accessibility, and equal rights for people with disabilities. They may advocate for policy changes, improved infrastructure, and better support services.

9. **Animal Advocates:** Advocates for animal welfare and rights work to protect and improve the treatment of animals. They may campaign against animal cruelty, promote adoption, and advocate for animal rights legislation.

Advocates often use a variety of strategies, including lobbying, public awareness campaigns, community organizing, legal action, and media engagement, to achieve their goals. Their work can significantly impact raising awareness, influencing public opinion, and driving positive change in society.

WHAT IS SELF-ADVOCACY?

Self-advocacy refers to an individual's ability to express their needs, preferences, and rights effectively, particularly in situations where they may face challenges or barriers. It involves speaking up for oneself, making informed decisions, and advocating for one's interests. Self-advocacy is especially important for individuals with disabilities, but it can apply to anyone in various aspects of life.

Key aspects of self-advocacy include:

1. **Awareness:** Self-advocacy begins with understanding one's needs, strengths, and weaknesses. It involves recognizing when you require assistance, accommodations, or support.

2. **Communication:** Effective self-advocacy requires clear and assertive communication. Individuals must be able to express their needs, concerns, and preferences confidently and respectfully.

3. **Knowledge:** Being informed about one's rights, responsibilities, and available resources is crucial. This includes understanding relevant laws, policies, and procedures.

4. **Decision-Making:** Self-advocates are actively involved in decision-making processes that affect their lives. They consider their options, make choices based on their preferences, and take responsibility for those decisions.

5. **Problem-Solving:** When faced with challenges or obstacles, self-advocates use problem-solving skills to identify solutions and overcome barriers.

6. **Assertiveness:** Self-advocacy often involves being assertive in advocating for one's rights and needs without being aggressive or passive. It is about standing up for oneself in a respectful manner.

7. **Negotiation:** In some cases, self-advocates may need to negotiate with others to reach mutually beneficial solutions. This can apply to situations like requesting accommodations in the workplace or discussing educational needs with teachers.

8. **Independence:** Self-advocacy fosters a sense of independence and self-reliance, empowering individuals to take an active role in their lives.

Self-advocacy can be particularly important for individuals with disabilities, as they may encounter barriers or discrimination in various aspects of life, including education, employment, healthcare, and social interactions. Advocating for necessary accommodations, equal opportunities, and access to services is essential for their full participation in society.

However, self-advocacy is a valuable skill for everyone, regardless of their abilities or circumstances. It can help individuals navigate various life situations, make informed choices, and have a voice in matters that affect them personally. Developing self-advocacy skills often involves education, practice, and support from trusted individuals or organizations that can provide guidance and resources.

THE DIFFERENCE BETWEEN SPECIAL EDUCATION SERVICES AND A 504 SERVICE PLAN

Special education and Section 504 plan accommodations are two distinct but related approaches to providing support and services to students with disabilities in the United States. While both aim to ensure that students with disabilities receive appropriate educational opportunities, their scope, eligibility criteria, and the services they offer differ.

Here is a breakdown of the key differences between special education (modifications) and Section 504 (accommodations):

Special Education Services (modifications):

1. **Eligibility Criteria:** To qualify for special education services, a student must have a disability that falls under one of the specific categories outlined in the Individuals with Disabilities Education Act (IDEA). These categories include conditions like specific learning disabilities, autism, intellectual disabilities, and more.

2. **Individualized Education Plan (IEP):** Students eligible for special education have an Individualized Education Plan (IEP) created specifically for them. The IEP outlines the student's unique needs, goals, and the services they will

receive. It may include curriculum modifications, instructional method changes, and other specialized services.

3. **Modifications:** In special education, modifications involve curriculum or educational program changes. These modifications are often significant and may include altering the content, pacing, or grading criteria to meet the student's individual needs. For example, a student with a learning disability might receive modified assignments or assessments.

4. **Legal Framework:** Special education is governed by federal law, primarily the Individuals with Disabilities Education Act (IDEA). IDEA provides a comprehensive framework for the provision of special education services, including evaluation, eligibility determination, and the creation of IEPs.

Section 504 Service Plan (accommodations):

1. **Eligibility Criteria:** Section 504 of the Rehabilitation Act of 1973 prohibits discrimination based on disability in programs and activities that receive federal funding. Unlike special education, Section 504 has a broader definition of disability, encompassing any physical or mental impairment that substantially limits one or more major life activities. This can include conditions like ADHD, anxiety disorders, and more.

2. **504 Service Plan:** Eligible students with disabilities are provided with a 504 Plan outlining the accommodations and support they will receive to ensure equal access to educational opportunities. Accommodations are adjustments or modifications to the environment (classroom), curriculum, or instructional methods to accommodate the student's needs.

3. **Accommodations:** Accommodations typically do not involve significant changes to the curriculum or grading criteria. Instead, they are designed to level the playing field by removing barriers to access and participation. For example, students with ADHD might receive extended time for tests or assignments, access to note-taking assistance, or preferential seating.

4. **Legal Framework:** Section 504 is a civil rights law that prohibits discrimination and applies not only to education but also to all federally funded programs and activities. Unlike IDEA, Section 504 does not provide funding for specialized services or dictate the specific services a student should receive. Instead, it ensures that students with disabilities have equal access and opportunities.

In summary, special education (modifications) is a more specialized and structured approach for students with disabilities who meet specific eligibility criteria under IDEA. At the same time, Section 504 (accommodations) provides a broader anti-discrimination framework to ensure equal access for individuals with disabilities in various settings, including education. Accommodations under Section 504 are typically designed to accommodate a student's disability without fundamentally altering the curriculum or program.

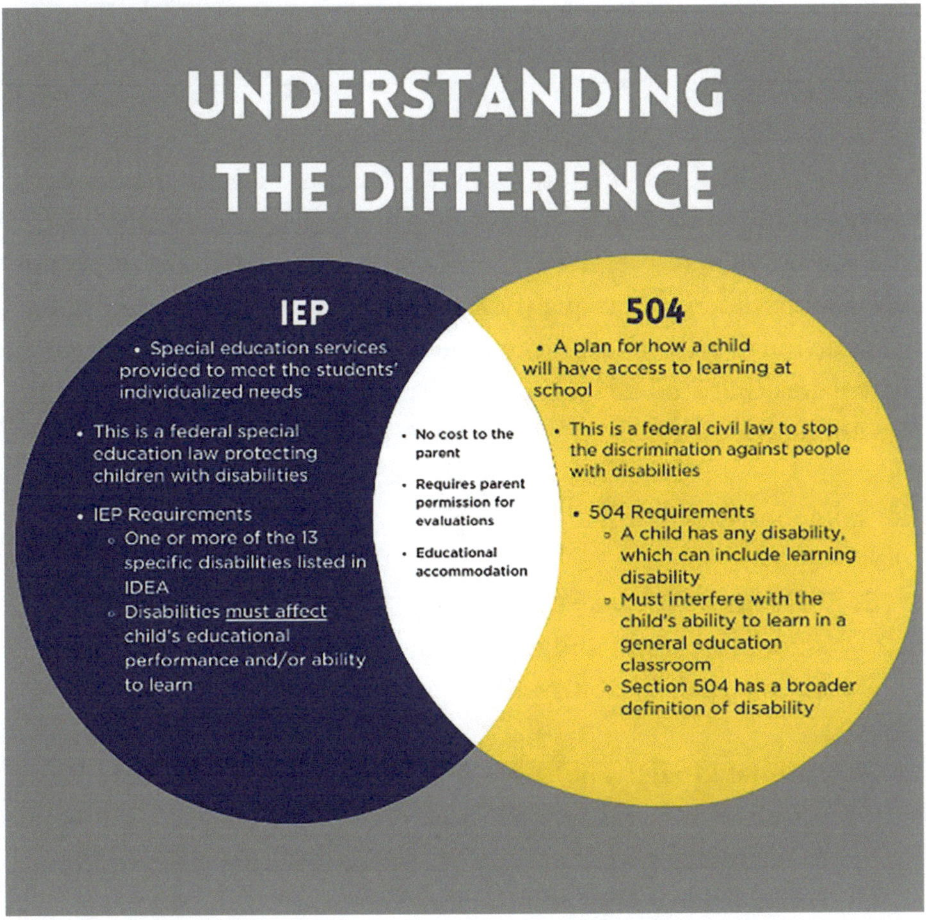
UNDERSTANDING THE DIFFERENCE
IEP
• Special education services provided to meet the students' individualized needs
• This is a federal special education law protecting children with disabilities
• IEP Requirements
◦ One or more of the 13 specific disabilities listed in IDEA
◦ Disabilities must affect child's educational performance and/or ability to learn
• No cost to the parent
• Requires parent permission for evaluations
• Educational accommodation
504
• A plan for how a child will have access to learning at school
• This is a federal civil law to stop the discrimination against people with disabilities
• 504 Requirements
◦ A child has any disability, which can include learning disability
◦ Must interfere with the child's ability to learn in a general education classroom
◦ Section 504 has a broader definition of disability

UNDERSTANDING THE INDIVIDUALIZED EDUCATION PROGRAM (IEP)

An Individualized Education Program (IEP) is a legally mandated document in the United States that outlines the specialized educational plan and services for a student with a disability. IEPs are created for students who qualify for special education services under the Individuals with Disabilities Education Act (IDEA). This federal law ensures that students with disabilities receive an appropriate and free public education.

Key components of an IEP typically include:

1. **Present Levels of Performance:** This section describes the student's current abilities, strengths, and weaknesses, as well as how their disability affects their learning.

2. **Annual Goals:** The IEP sets specific, measurable goals for the student to achieve within a year. These goals are tailored to address the student's unique needs and can cover academic, social, behavioral, and functional areas.

3. **Special Education and Related Services:** The IEP outlines the specialized services and support the student will receive. This may include services like speech therapy, occupational therapy, counseling, or adaptive physical education.

4. **Accommodations and Modifications:** The IEP specifies any accommodations and modifications that will be provided to help the student access the general education curriculum. Accommodations might include extended time for tests, preferential seating, or assistive technology.

5. **Participation in General Education:** The IEP outlines the extent to which the student will participate in the general education setting. It may specify whether the student will be fully included, partially included, or spend most of their time in a special education setting.

6. **Transition Services:** For students of transition age (typically 16 and older), the IEP includes transition planning to prepare the student for life after high school. This can consist of vocational training, job placement services, and independent living skills.

7. **Assessment:** The IEP describes how the student's progress will be measured and how often progress reports will be provided to parents or guardians.

8. **Placement:** The document specifies the educational placement of the student, which may be in a regular classroom, special education classroom, or a combination of both.

9. **Parental Involvement:** Parents or guardians are actively involved in developing and reviewing the IEP. Their input is essential in creating a plan that best meets students' needs.

10. **Timeline and Review:** The IEP includes a timeline for reviewing and updating the plan. Typically, it is reviewed annually, but it can be more frequent if needed.

The IEP is a collaborative effort involving educators, special education professionals, parents or guardians, and often the student (if age-appropriate). Its purpose is to ensure that students with disabilities receive an individualized and appropriate education tailored to their specific needs, allowing them to access the general curriculum and make educational progress. It also provides a legal framework to protect the educational rights of students with disabilities.

UNDERSTANDING THE 504 SERVICE PLAN

A 504 Plan, also known as a Section 504 Plan, is a document created to provide accommodations and support services to students with disabilities in the United States who do not qualify for special education services under the Individuals with Disabilities Education Act (IDEA). Instead of being governed by IDEA, 504 Plans are established under Section 504 of the Rehabilitation Act of 1973, a federal law prohibiting discrimination based on disability in programs and activities receiving federal financial assistance.

Here are the key aspects of a 504 Service Plan:

1. **Eligibility:** To qualify for a 504 Plan, a student must have a physical or mental impairment that substantially limits one or more major life activities, such as walking, seeing, hearing, learning, or concentrating. The disability must impact the student's ability to access and participate in the school environment.

2. **Evaluation:** A team, typically including parents or guardians, teachers, and school staff, evaluates the student to determine eligibility for a 504 Plan. The evaluation assesses the nature and extent of the student's disability and its impact on their education.

3. **Accommodations:** The 504 Plan outlines the specific accommodations and support services the student will receive to ensure equal access to educational opportunities. These accommodations can vary widely depending on the student's needs but may include extended time for tests, preferential seating, access to assistive technology, or adjustments in classroom instruction.

4. **Regular Education Setting:** Unlike special education, which often involves specialized instruction and curriculum modifications, 504 Plans focus on removing barriers in the regular education setting. The goal is to provide the support that allows the student to participate fully in the general education curriculum.

5. **Development and Implementation:** The 504 Plan is developed collaboratively by the school team, including parents or guardians, and is tailored to the student's specific needs. Once created, the plan is implemented in the school environment, and teachers and staff are responsible for providing accommodations.

6. **Review and Revision:** 504 Plans should be reviewed periodically to assess the student's progress and adjust accommodations as needed. While there is no specific requirement for how often a plan should be reviewed, regular assessments are essential to ensure that the student's needs continue to be met.

7. **Parental Involvement:** Parents or guardians are typically involved in developing and reviewing the 504 Plan. Their input is essential in determining the appropriate accommodations and addressing their child's needs.

504 Plans are designed to provide students with disabilities equal access to educational opportunities while allowing them to remain in the general education environment to the maximum extent possible. These plans are not limited to academic settings and can extend to other school activities, such as extracurriculars, field trips, and sports. The focus is on creating a supportive and inclusive educational environment for students with disabilities.

TEA INDIVIDUALIZED EDUCATION PROGRAM (IEP) OPTIONS AND CODES

IEP options and codes

The Texas Education Agency (TEA) provides guidelines and templates for Individualized Education Programs (IEPs) in Texas. While specific options and codes may vary among school districts, TEA offers a standardized format and guidance for IEP development. Below are some common elements you might find in a Texas IEP:

1. **Eligibility Category Codes:** Texas uses eligibility category codes to specify the primary disability category under which a student qualifies for special education services.

   Standard eligibility category codes in Texas include:

   SLD: Specific Learning Disability
   OHI: Other Health Impairment
   ASD: Autism Spectrum Disorder
   ID: Intellectual Disability
   ED: Emotional Disturbance
   VI: Visual Impairment
   HI: Hearing Impairment
   TBI: Traumatic Brain Injury
   SI: Speech OR Language Impairment
   AI: Auditory Impairment

2. **Annual Goals and Objectives:** Each goal and objective in the Texas IEP typically has its unique code or identifier. These codes are used to reference specific goals and track progress over time. For example, a goal related to reading fluency might have a code like "Goal 1.1."

3. **Services and Accommodations Codes:** The IEP may list the specific services and accommodations a student will receive. These codes can vary but are typically used to denote services such as speech therapy (SP), occupational therapy (OT), physical therapy (PT), or accommodations like extended time on tests (EXT) or preferential seating (PS).

4. **Placement Codes:** Texas IEPs often specify the educational placement for the student.

   Standard placement codes include:

   GENED: General Education Placement
   SPED: Special Education Placement
   INCL: Inclusive Settings (a combination of general and special education)
   RES: Resource Setting (support in a special education classroom)

5. **Assessment Codes:** Texas IEPs may include codes to specify the assessments or evaluations that will be conducted to measure the student's progress or determine eligibility. Examples include "WISC-V" for the Wechsler Intelligence Scale for Children, Fifth Edition, or "WIAT-III" for the Wechsler Individual Achievement Test, Third Edition.

6. **Frequency and Duration Codes:** Some Texas IEPs include codes to specify how often and for how long certain services or accommodations will be provided. For instance, "OT-2x/week for 30 minutes" indicates occupational therapy twice a week for 30 minutes each session.

7. **Transition Services Codes:** For students of transition age (typically 16 and older), the IEP may include codes related to transition planning, such as "EMP" for employment services, "INDLIV" for independent living skills, or "POSTSEC" for post-secondary education planning.

It is important to note that while TEA provides guidance and templates for IEP development in Texas, the specific codes and options used in an IEP may vary among school districts. Parents, guardians, and educators should work collaboratively to understand and document the student's needs and goals within the framework provided by TEA and their specific school or district's policies.

504 service plan option and codes

Unlike Individualized Education Programs (IEPs), which have specific codes and standardized templates in many states, 504 Plans do not typically use specific codes or templates similarly. Instead, 504 Plans are more flexible and individualized to meet the unique needs of each student with a disability. The focus of a 504 Plan is on providing accommodations and modifications that ensure equal access to educational opportunities rather than using standardized codes.

Below are some standard accommodations and modifications that might be included in a 504 Service Plan, along with descriptions, though standardized codes do not represent these:

1. **Extended Time on Tests and Assignments:** This accommodation gives students extra time to complete tests, quizzes, or assignments. It can be particularly helpful for students who need help with time management or processing information quickly.

2. **Frequent Breaks:** Some students benefit from frequent short breaks during instruction or assessments to help them maintain focus and attention.

3. **Preferential Seating:** Placing a student with a disability in a specific location in the classroom, such as near the teacher or away from distractions, can be designated in a 504 Plan.

4. **Use of Assistive Technology:** The plan might specify the use of assistive technology devices or software to support the student's learning or communication needs.

5. **Alternative Testing Formats:** This accommodation can include providing tests in alternative formats, such as audio versions, large print, or braille, depending on the student's needs.

6. **Note-Taking Support:** Students with disabilities may receive accommodations related to note-taking, such as access to class notes or using a scribe.

7. **Modified Assignments:** For some students, assignments may be modified in terms of content, length, or complexity to make them more accessible.

8. **Behavioral Supports:** Behavioral supports and strategies may be included in the plan to help students with emotional or behavioral challenges.

9. **Access to a 504 Coordinator:** The plan may specify that the student or parent can contact a designated 504 Coordinator at the school to discuss concerns or requests for accommodations.

10. **Accessibility Modifications:** Schools may make physical accessibility modifications *as needed* for students with mobility impairments.

While no standardized codes exist for these accommodations and modifications in a 504 Plan, the plan should clearly describe each accommodation, how it will be implemented, and any other relevant details. 504 Plans are highly individualized, so the specific accommodations and modifications will vary based on the student's unique needs as determined through an evaluation process. Parents, guardians, students, and school staff should collaborate to develop and document the specific accommodations and modifications that best support the student's access to education.

THE DIFFERENCES

Individualized Education Programs (IEPs) and 504 plans can offer formal help for K–12 students struggling in school. They are similar in some ways but very different in others.

The following chart compares them side by side to help you understand the differences. (Lee, 2023).

	IEP	504 plan
Basic description	A blueprint or plan for a child's **special education** experience at school.	A blueprint or plan for how the school will provide support and remove barriers for a student with a disability.
What it does	Provides individualized special education and related services to meet a child's unique needs. These services are provided at no cost to families.	Provides services and changes to the learning environment to enable students to learn alongside their peers. As with an IEP, a 504 plan is provided at no cost to families.
What law applies	The Individuals with Disabilities Education Act (IDEA): This is a federal special education law for children with disabilities.	Section 504 of the Rehabilitation Act of 1973: This is a federal civil rights law to stop discrimination against people with disabilities.
Who's eligible	To get an IEP, there are two requirements: A child has one or more of the **13 disabilities** listed in IDEA. The law lists specific challenges, like learning disabilities, ADHD, autism, and others. **And** the disability must affect the child's educational performance and/or ability to learn and benefit from the general education curriculum. The child must need specialized instruction to make progress in school.	To get a 504 plan, there are two requirements: A child has *any* disability. Section 504 covers a wide range of different struggles in school. **And** the disability must interfere with the child's ability to learn in a general education classroom. Section 504 has a broader definition of a disability than IDEA. (It says a disability must substantially limit one or more basic life activities. This can include learning, reading, communicating, and thinking.) That's why a child who doesn't qualify for an IEP might still be able to get a 504 plan.
Independent educational evaluation	Families can ask the school district to pay for an independent educational evaluation (IEE) by an outside expert. The district doesn't have to agree. Families can always pay for an outside evaluation themselves, but the district may not give it much weight.	Doesn't allow families to ask for an IEE. As with an IEP evaluation, families can always pay for an outside evaluation themselves.
Who creates it	There are strict legal requirements about who participates. With a few exceptions, the entire IEP team must be present for IEP meetings. The team must include: • The child's parent or caregiver • At least one of the child's general education teachers • At least one special education teacher • A school psychologist or other specialist who can interpret evaluation results • A district representative with authority over special education services	The rules about who's on the 504 team are less specific than they are for an IEP. A 504 plan is created by a team of people who are familiar with the child and who understand the evaluation data and special services options. This might include: • The child's parent or caregiver • General and special education teachers • The school principal

What's in it	The IEP sets learning goals and describes the services the school will provide. It's a written document. Here are some of the most important things the IEP must include: • The child's present levels of academic and functional performance — how the child is currently doing in school • Annual education goals for the child and how the school will track progress • The services the child will get — this may include special education, related, supplementary, and extended school year services • The timing of services — when they start, how often they occur, and how long they last • Any accommodations — changes to the child's learning environment • Any modifications — changes to what the child is expected to learn or know • How the child will participate in standardized tests • How the child will be included in general education classes and school activities	There is no standard 504 plan. Unlike an IEP, a 504 plan doesn't *have* to be a written document. A 504 plan generally includes the following: • Specific accommodations, supports, or services for the child • Names of who will provide each service • Name of the person responsible for ensuring the plan is implemented
Notice	When the school wants to change a child's services or placement, it has to tell families in writing *before* the change. This is called **prior written notice**. Notice is also required for any IEP meetings and evaluations. Families also have **"stay put" rights** to keep services in place while there's a disagreement about the IEP.	The school must notify families about an evaluation or a "significant change" in placement. Notice doesn't have to be in writing, but most schools do so anyway.
Consent	A parent or caregiver must consent in writing for the school to evaluate a child. They must also consent in writing before the school can provide the services in an IEP.	A parent or caregiver's consent is required for the school district to evaluate a child.
How often it's reviewed and revised	The IEP team must review the IEP at least once a year. The child must be reevaluated every three years to determine whether services are still needed.	The rules vary by state. Generally, a 504 plan is reviewed each year and a reevaluation is done every three years or when needed.
How to resolve disputes	IDEA gives families several **ways to resolve disputes** (usually in this order): • Mediation • Due process complaint • Resolution session • Civil lawsuit • State complaint • Lawsuit	Section 504 gives families several **options for resolving disagreements** with the school: • Mediation • Alternative dispute resolution • Impartial hearing • Complaint to the Office for Civil Rights (OCR) • Lawsuit
Funding/costs	Students receive these services at no charge. States receive additional funding for students with IEPs.	Students receive these services at no charge. States do not receive extra funding for students with 504 plans. But the federal government can take funding away from programs (including schools) that don't meet their legal duty to serve kids with disabilities. IDEA funds can't be used to serve students with 504 plans.

SIX MYTHS ABOUT 504 SERVICE PLANS

Myth #1: A 504 plan is the same as an IEP.

Fact: Both 504 plans and IEPs can help kids thrive in school. However, they are covered by different laws and work differently. The point of a 504 plan is to give a child equal access to learning at school. An IEP, on the other hand, is focused on special education services (Lee, 2023).

Myth #2: A 504 plan is not as good as an IEP.

Fact: A good plan is the one that fits a child's needs. A child with severe learning challenges probably needs special education through an IEP. However, another child doing OK in school may only need specific accommodations through a 504 plan. And some kids, even those who learn and think differently, do not need a formal plan (Lee, 2023).

Myth #3: A 504 plan can only give accommodations, not services.

Fact: Some people think that a 504 plan cannot include services. But that's not true. The U.S. Department of Education says a 504 plan *can* include school services. For example, some 504 plans offer things like speech therapy or study skills classes. It is less common, however.

The services a 504 plan offers may not be the same as those available in an IEP (Lee, 2023).

Myth #4: Students can't get 504 accommodations for advanced or AP classes.

Fact: There are many kids with 504 plans who are in advanced or AP classes. Kids who learn and think differently can even be gifted. A child with a 504 plan in an advanced class has the same rights as in other classes — the right to equal access to learning. This may mean accommodations, like text-to-speech technology or extra time for assignments.

Myth #5: 504 plans are for kids with ADHD.

Fact: 504 plans are not just for one type of challenge or difficulty. Some kids with 504 plans have ADHD. Some have learning disabilities. Others may have severe allergies, trouble with mobility, or other challenges. Keep in mind, too, that some kids with ADHD are eligible for IEPs, not just 504 plans (Lee, 2023).

Myth #6: There are 504 plans in college.

Fact: There are no IEPs or 504 plans in college. Students who qualify do have the right to accommodations in college. But it won't be through a 504 plan. Colleges also have different requirements for getting accommodations. And in college, students (not the school) are responsible for asking for accommodations (Lee, 2023).

ELEMENTARY K–6

I HAVE AN IEP TO RECEIVE SPECIAL EDUCATION SERVICES, NOW WHAT?

An Individualized Education Program (IEP) for kindergarten through sixth-grade students is a specialized educational plan tailored to meet the unique needs of a student with a disability in the elementary school setting. The content and components of an IEP can vary based on the student's specific needs, but here is a general framework for developing an IEP for students in this grade range:

1. **Student Information:**

   - Include the student's name, date of birth, grade level, and school information.
   - Specify the primary disability category under which the student qualifies for special education services (e.g., Specific Learning Disability, Autism Spectrum Disorder, Speech or Language Impairment).

2. **Present Levels of Academic Achievement and Functional Performance:**

   - Describe the student's current academic and functional abilities, including strengths and weaknesses.
   - Explain how the disability affects the student's involvement and progress in the general education curriculum and school activities.

3. **Measurable Annual Goals:**

    - Outline specific, measurable, and attainable academic and functional goals for the student to achieve within a year.
    - Goals should address areas of need such as reading, math, communication, social skills, behavior, or motor skills.
    - Goals should be broken down into short-term objectives or benchmarks, especially for younger students.

4. **Special Education and Related Services:**

    - Specify the special education services the student will receive. This may include:
    - The type and frequency of services (e.g., speech therapy, occupational therapy, special education instruction).
    - The location of services (e.g., in the general education classroom, a resource room, or a separate special education setting).
    - Describe related services like counseling or physical therapy, if applicable.

5. **Accommodations and Modifications:**

    - List the accommodations and modifications that will be provided to support the student's access to the general education curriculum.
    - Common accommodations may include extended time on tests, preferential seating, access to assistive technology, and modified assignments.

6. **Participation in General Education:**

   - Specify the extent to which the student will participate in the general education setting. Indicate if the student will be fully included, partially included, or spend most of their time in special education.

7. **Transition Services (if applicable):**

   - For students in the upper elementary grades (fourth, fifth, or sixth), include transition goals and services related to preparing the student for middle school or beyond. This might involve career exploration, vocational training, or independent living skills.

8. **Assessment and Progress Monitoring:**

   - Describe how the student's progress will be measured and how often progress reports will be provided to parents or guardians.
   - Include information about the assessments or evaluations used to measure the student's progress.

9. **Parent and Student Participation:**

   - Document the involvement of parents or guardians in the development of the IEP.
   - Encourage and specify the role of the student in their educational planning, especially as they become more involved in decision-making in the upper elementary grades.

10. **Review and Revision:**

- Specify how often the IEP will be reviewed and revised. Typically, IEPs are reviewed annually, but more frequent reviews may sometimes be necessary.

Remember that an IEP is a collaborative effort involving educators, special education professionals, parents or guardians, and, when appropriate, the student. It should be a dynamic document that evolves to meet the changing needs of the students as they progress through elementary school.

WHAT IS THE PURPOSE OF MY BEHAVIOR INTERVENTION PLAN (BIP)?

A behavior intervention plan for elementary students, often referred to as a Behavior Intervention Plan (BIP), is a structured and individualized document designed to address and manage challenging behaviors exhibited by a student in an elementary school setting. The primary goal of a BIP is to promote positive behavior while reducing or eliminating problem behaviors that interfere with the student's learning and the learning environment.

Here are the key components of a behavior intervention plan for elementary students:

1. **Behavior Assessment:** A thorough assessment of the student's behavior is conducted before developing a BIP. This may involve gathering data, conducting observations, and seeking input from teachers, parents, and other relevant individuals. The assessment helps identify the specific problem behaviors, their triggers, and patterns of occurrence.

2. **Clear Behavior Definitions:** The behavior plan should provide clear and concise definitions of the target behaviors. It is essential to describe what the behaviors look like and when they occur to ensure consistency in identifying and addressing them.

3. **Positive Behavior Goals:** The BIP should outline specific, measurable, and achievable goals for improving the student's behavior. These goals should focus on promoting positive behaviors that are desirable and appropriate in the school environment.

4. **Targeted Interventions:** The plan should detail the strategies and interventions that will be implemented to address the challenging behaviors. These interventions should be evidence-based and selected based on their appropriateness for the individual student.

5. **Functional Behavior Assessment (FBA):** In some cases, a more in-depth FBA may be conducted to analyze the function or purpose of the problem behaviors. Understanding why a student engages in certain behaviors can guide the selection of effective interventions.

6. **Teaching Replacement Behaviors:** Instead of solely focusing on eliminating problem behaviors, the BIP should include strategies for teaching the student alternative. These more appropriate behaviors serve the same function as the problem behaviors.

7. **Supports and Strategies:** The plan should identify the supports and strategies provided to the student. These may include visual supports, social skills training, self-regulation techniques, or environmental modifications.

8. **Response to Behavior:** The BIP should specify how staff will respond when the student exhibits the target behaviors. This may involve planned consequences, redirection, or de-escalation techniques.

9. **Data Collection and Progress Monitoring:** The behavior plan should include a system for ongoing data collection to monitor the student's progress toward meeting the behavior goals. This information helps determine the effectiveness of the interventions and whether adjustments are needed.

10. **Team Collaboration:** Collaboration among school staff, parents or guardians, and relevant specialists (i.e., behavior analysts or school psychologists) is crucial. All team members should work together to implement the plan consistently and effectively.

11. **Crisis Intervention:** If the student's behavior poses a risk to themselves or others, the plan should outline crisis intervention procedures to ensure the safety of everyone involved.

12. **Regular Review and Revision:** The BIP is not a static document. It should be reviewed regularly to assess progress and make necessary adjustments to the interventions and goals.

13. **Consistency and Communication:** Communication among school staff is essential to ensure that interventions are applied consistently across different settings and with different individuals working with the student.

It is important to note that a behavior plan should focus on positive behavioral support, teaching appropriate skills, and creating a supportive and inclusive environment. Additionally, it should comply with applicable laws and regulations, including those related to special education and students with disabilities.

WHAT IS IN THE BEHAVIOR INTERVENTION PLAN (BIP)?

A Behavior Intervention Plan (BIP) for elementary students (K-6) is designed to address specific challenging behaviors exhibited by students in the school setting. The plan includes strategies and interventions to promote positive behavior and reduce or eliminate problem behaviors. Below are examples of components you might find in a BIP for an elementary student:

Student Information:

- Student Name: [Student's Name]
- Date of Birth: [Date of Birth]
- Grade: [Grade]
- School: [School Name]
- Primary Disability: [Specify the primary disability category, if applicable]

Behavior Definitions:

- Problem Behavior: [Describe the target problem behavior(s) in clear and observable terms]
- Frequency: [How often does the behavior occur?]
- Duration: [How long does the behavior typically last?]
- Triggers: [Identify specific antecedents or triggers that precede the behavior]

Positive Behavior Goals:

- Goal 1: Increase [Specify a positive behavior goal, e.g., on-task behavior] to [desired level, e.g., 90%] during [specified time frame, e.g., math class].
- Goal 2: Decrease [Specify a problem behavior] to [desired level] during [specified time frame].

Functional Behavior Assessment (FBA):

- Summarize the results of the FBA, including identified functions of the problem behavior (e.g., attention-seeking, escape).

Targeted Interventions:

- Intervention 1: Implement a token economy system to reinforce positive behavior. The student will earn tokens for on-task behavior and can exchange them for preferred activities.
- Intervention 2: Provide clear visual schedules and prompts to help the student transition between activities and reduce anxiety.
- Intervention 3: Teach the student self-regulation strategies, such as deep breathing exercises, to use when feeling overwhelmed.

Teaching Replacement Behaviors:

- *Replacement Behavior 1*: Teach the student to request a break when feeling overwhelmed instead of engaging in problem behavior.

- *Replacement Behavior 2*: Teach the student to use a "calm down" corner with sensory tools when feeling agitated instead of leaving the classroom.

Supports and Strategies:

- Visual Supports: Implement visual supports, including visual schedules, social stories, and visual cues, to help the student understand expectations.
- Social Skills Training: Conduct weekly social skills training sessions to improve the student's ability to interact with peers appropriately.
- Environmental Modifications: Create a structured classroom environment with clear routines and minimal distractions.

Response to Behavior:

- When the student exhibits the problem behavior, staff will use a "three-strike" system:
- **Strike 1**: Verbal redirection and reminder of expectations.
- **Strike 2**: Brief time-out to the "calm down" corner.
- **Strike 3**: Meeting with the school counselor to discuss strategies.

Data Collection and Progress Monitoring:

- Data on behavior frequency and duration will be collected daily during [specified times].
- Progress toward behavior goals will be reviewed weekly during team meetings.

Team Collaboration:

- Collaboration among the student's teacher, special education staff, school counselor, and parents is essential to ensure consistency in implementing the BIP.

Crisis Intervention:

- If the student's behavior poses an immediate safety risk, staff will follow the crisis intervention protocol outlined in the school's crisis management plan.

Regular Review and Revision:

- The BIP will be reviewed and, if necessary, revised at least once a month to assess progress and adjust as needed.

Consistency and Communication:

- Ongoing communication among school staff will ensure that interventions are applied consistently across settings and with different personnel working with the student.

Please note that the examples provided are general guidelines, and a specific BIP should be developed in collaboration with a team of professionals, including educators, behavior specialists, and parents or guardians, to meet the student's individualized needs. Additionally, BIPs should adhere to all applicable laws and regulations, including those related to special education and students with disabilities.

WHAT DO I NEED TO KNOW ABOUT MY BEHAVIOR IMPLEMENTATION PLAN?

Elementary students do not typically self-identify the need for a Behavior Intervention Plan (BIP) on their own, as a team typically makes the decision to create a BIP of educators, specialists, and parents or guardians. However, students may exhibit signs or behaviors that suggest they could benefit from a BIP. Adults, including teachers and school professionals, are responsible for recognizing these signs and initiating the process of developing a BIP. Here are some indications that an elementary student may need a BIP:

1. **Consistent Challenging Behaviors:** The student displays persistent and challenging behaviors that interfere with their learning, the learning of others, or the overall school environment. These behaviors may include aggression, noncompliance, disruptions, or emotional outbursts.

2. **Failure to Respond to Universal Interventions:** The student has yet to show significant improvement in behavior despite the implementation of school-wide or classroom-wide behavior interventions and supports, such as a positive behavior support system or classroom management strategies.

3. **Safety Concerns:** The student's behaviors pose a safety risk to themselves, peers, or school staff. This may include physical

aggression, self-injurious behaviors, or elopement (running away).

4. **Impact on Academic Progress:** Challenging behaviors negatively impact the student's academic progress and ability to access the general education curriculum. These behaviors may result in missed instruction time or disruptions during lessons.

5. **Consistency of Problem Behaviors:** The student's challenging behaviors occur consistently across different settings (e.g., classroom, cafeteria, playground) and with different adults, suggesting that the issues are not isolated incidents.

6. **Limited Response to Consequences:** The student does not appear to respond to typical consequences or discipline strategies, such as time-outs or loss of privileges.

7. **Parent or Guardian Concerns:** Parents or guardians may express concerns about their child's behavior at school and request additional support.

8. **Data Collection:** Data collection and behavior tracking indicate a consistent pattern of problem behaviors that need to be addressed through targeted interventions.

If an elementary student exhibits one or more of these signs, it is essential for school professionals to collaborate with parents or guardians to assess the situation. This may involve conducting a Functional Behavior Assessment (FBA) to better understand the function or purpose of the problem behaviors. Based on the results of the FBA, a team can determine whether the student would benefit from a Behavior Intervention Plan (BIP).

A BIP is a comprehensive plan designed to provide targeted interventions and support to address challenging behaviors and promote positive behavior change. It should be developed with input from all relevant stakeholders, including the student's parents or guardians, and should be regularly reviewed and adjusted based on the student's progress.

How do I know that I need a BIP or an IEP?

Recognizing the signs that an elementary student may need both an Individualized Education Program (IEP) and a Behavior Intervention Plan (BIP) is essential to ensure that the student receives the appropriate support for their educational and behavioral needs. Here are some signs that may indicate the need for both an IEP and a BIP:

Signs that an elementary student may need an IEP:

1. **Academic Struggles:** The student consistently performs below grade level in one or more academic areas, such as reading, math, writing, or communication skills.

2. **Learning Disabilities:** A student may show signs of a specific learning disability, such as difficulty with reading (dyslexia), writing (dysgraphia), or math (dyscalculia).

3. **Speech or Language Delays:** The student has significant speech or language delays that impact their ability to communicate effectively.

4. **Developmental Delays:** Signs of developmental delays, including motor skills, social-emotional development, or cognitive functioning, may warrant consideration for an IEP.

5. **Attention and Focus Issues:** A student struggles with attention, concentration, and maintaining focus in the classroom, potentially indicating attention-deficit/ hyperactivity disorder (ADHD).

6. **Behavioral Challenges:** Problematic behaviors in the classroom that significantly disrupt learning may be a sign of underlying issues that need to be addressed through an IEP.

7. **Emotional or Behavioral Disorders:** Persistent emotional or behavioral difficulties that interfere with the student's social and emotional well-being may require specialized support.

8. **Communication and Interaction Difficulties:** Students with difficulty with social interactions, understanding social cues, or forming relationships may have autism spectrum disorder (ASD) or related conditions.

Signs that an elementary student may need a BIP (in addition to an IEP):

1. **Challenging Behaviors:** The student exhibits challenging behaviors that are disruptive, aggressive, self-injurious, or unsafe for themselves or others.

2. **Consistency of Problem Behaviors:** The problematic behaviors occur consistently across different settings and with different adults, suggesting the need for targeted interventions.

3. **Failure to Respond to Universal Interventions:** The student does not respond to school-wide or classroom-wide behavior interventions and supports designed for all students.

4. **Safety Concerns:** Problem behaviors pose a safety risk to the student, peers, or school staff, necessitating specific interventions to ensure safety.

5. **Impact on Learning:** Challenging behaviors significantly impede the student's ability to access and benefit from educational instruction.

6. **Data and Assessment Results:** Data collection and behavioral assessments indicate a consistent pattern of problem behaviors that require targeted intervention strategies.

It is important to note that the decision to initiate an IEP or a BIP should involve a collaborative and multidisciplinary approach. School professionals, including teachers, special education staff, behavior specialists, and administrators, should work together with parents or guardians to assess the student's needs comprehensively. The development and implementation of an IEP and BIP should be based on a thorough evaluation of the student's strengths, weaknesses, and individualized needs to ensure they receive appropriate and effective support.

WHAT QUESTION SHOULD I ASK MY CHILD'S TEACHER ABOUT THE IEP?

When considering whether an elementary student may need an Individualized Education Program (IEP), it is important for parents or guardians to have open and constructive communication with the child's teacher. Asking the right questions can help gather information and insights about the student's educational needs.

Here are some examples of questions to ask the elementary teacher:

1. **What are my child's strengths and weaknesses in the classroom?**

    - This question can help you understand your child's academic and behavioral profile.

2. **Have you noticed any consistent academic challenges my child is facing?**

    - Understanding specific academic struggles can provide insights into potential learning disabilities or areas where additional support may be needed.

3. **Does my child receive any special accommodations or interventions in the classroom?**

    - Knowing what accommodations are already in place can help assess whether additional support is needed.

4. **How does my child interact with peers and adults in the classroom?**

    - Information about social interactions and behavior can be important, especially if there are concerns about social-emotional development.

5. **Have there been any significant changes in my child's behavior or performance in the classroom?**

    - Changes in behavior or performance may indicate underlying issues that need attention.

6. **What strategies or interventions have been implemented to address my child's challenges?**

    - Understanding the strategies that have been tried can help you gauge their effectiveness.

7. **Is my child meeting grade-level expectations in core subjects like reading, math, and writing?**

    - Assessing grade-level proficiency can indicate whether additional support is needed.

8. **Has my child been assessed for any learning disabilities or developmental delays?**

    - Knowing whether assessments have been conducted can guide discussions about potential evaluations.

9. **Are there concerns about my child's attention or focus in the classroom?**

    - Attention and focus issues can impact learning and may warrant consideration for evaluation.

10. **Do you think my child may benefit from more individualized support, such as an IEP or a 504 Plan?**

    - This question directly addresses the need for specialized services and opens the door to further discussion.

11. **What can I do at home to support my child's learning and development?**

    - Teachers can provide suggestions for reinforcing skills and addressing challenges outside of school.

12. **Can we schedule a meeting to discuss my child's needs further, including the possibility of an evaluation for an IEP?**

    - Requesting a meeting is an important step in initiating the evaluation process.

Remember that the teacher's input is valuable, but the decision to pursue an IEP should be based on a collaborative process involving educators, specialists, and parents or guardians. Suppose there are concerns about a student's educational needs. In that case, it may be appropriate to request an evaluation by the school district's special education team to determine eligibility for special education services, including the development of an IEP.

WHAT QUESTION SHOULD I ASK MY TEACHER ABOUT A 504 SERVICE PLAN?

When considering whether an elementary student may need a 504 Plan, its important for parents or guardians to engage in a productive conversation with the child's teacher. A 504 Plan provides accommodations and support to students with disabilities who do not qualify for special education services under an Individualized Education Program (IEP).

Here are some examples of questions to ask the elementary teacher about the need for a 504 Service Plan:

1. **What specific challenges or barriers has my child been facing in the classroom?**

    - Understanding the specific challenges your child is experiencing is essential for determining the need for accommodations.

2. **Have you observed any consistent patterns of behavior or difficulties that may be related to a disability?**

    - Identifying patterns of behavior or challenges can help pinpoint areas where accommodations may be beneficial.

3. **Are there any documented medical or educational diagnoses that may impact my child's ability to access and benefit from education?**

- If your child has a diagnosed condition or medical issue, it's important to discuss how it affects their educational experience.

4. **Has my child been receiving any accommodations or support in the classroom?**

   - Knowing if any informal accommodations have been implemented can provide insights into potential 504 Plan accommodations.

5. **Do you think my child may benefit from formal accommodations to ensure equal access to educational opportunities?**

   - This question directly addresses the need for a 504 Plan and invites the teacher's input.

6. **Are there any specific accommodations or strategies that you believe would be helpful for my child?**

   - The teacher's suggestions for accommodations can guide discussions with the school's 504 Plan coordinator.

7. **How do my child's challenges impact their academic performance and overall school experience?**

   - Understanding the impact of the challenges on your child's education is important for making informed decisions.

8. **Is it possible to schedule a meeting with the school's 504 Plan coordinator to discuss my child's needs and potential accommodations?**

   - Requesting a meeting with the 504 Plan coordinator is a crucial step in the process of developing a 504 Plan.

9. **Are there any relevant assessments or documentation that can support the need for a 504 Plan?**

   - In some cases, assessments or documentation may be necessary to establish the need for accommodations.

10. **What can I do at home to support my child's learning and address their challenges?**

    - The teacher may have suggestions for how you can support your child's education outside of school.

11. **Can you provide examples of how specific accommodations might help my child succeed in the classroom?**

    - Concrete examples of accommodations can help you understand their potential impact.

Remember that developing a 504 Plan involves collaboration between parents or guardians, school staff, and the school's 504 coordinator. If there is agreement that a 504 Plan is necessary, the process will typically include an evaluation to determine eligibility and the specific accommodations that will be included in the plan.

SECONDARY 7-12

I HAVE AN IEP TO RECEIVE SPECIAL EDUCATION SERVICES, NOW WHAT?

An Individualized Education Program (IEP) for grades 7-12 is a specialized educational plan designed to meet the unique needs of a student with a disability in a middle school or high school setting. The content and components of an IEP can vary based on the student's specific needs, but here is a general framework for developing an IEP for students in this grade range:

Student Information:

- Include the student's name, date of birth, grade level, and school information.
- Specify the primary disability category under which the student qualifies for special education services (e.g., Specific Learning Disability, Autism Spectrum Disorder, Emotional Disturbance).

Present Levels of Academic Achievement and Functional Performance:

- Describe the student's current academic and functional abilities, including strengths and weaknesses.
- Explain how the disability affects the student's involvement and progress in the general education curriculum and school activities.

Measurable Annual Goals:

- Outline specific, measurable, and attainable academic and functional goals for the student to achieve within a year.
- Goals should address areas such as reading, math, communication, social skills, behavior, or vocational skills.
- Goals should align with the student's post-secondary transition plans.

Special Education and Related Services:

- Specify the special education services the student will receive.
- The type and frequency of services (e.g., specialized instruction, speech therapy, occupational therapy).
- The location of services (e.g., in the general education classroom, a resource room, or a separate special education setting).
- Describe related services like counseling or assistive technology, if applicable.

Accommodations and Modifications:

- List the accommodations and modifications that will be provided to support the student's access to the general education curriculum.
- Accommodations may include extended time on tests, access to assistive technology, or preferential seating.

Participation in General Education:

- Specify the extent to which the student will participate in the general education setting. Indicate if the student will be fully included, partially included, or spend most of their time in special education.

Transition Services:

- For students in grades 9-12, include transition goals and services related to post-secondary planning, such as career exploration, vocational training, and independent living skills.

Assessment and Progress Monitoring:

- Describe how the student's progress will be measured and how often progress reports will be provided to parents or guardians.
- Include information about the assessments or evaluations used to measure the student's progress.

Parent and Student Participation:

- Document the involvement of parents or guardians in the development of the IEP.
- Encourage and specify the role of the student in their own educational planning, particularly as they become more involved in decision-making in the upper grades.

Review and Revision:

- Specify how often the IEP will be reviewed and revised. Typically, IEPs are reviewed annually, but more frequent reviews may sometimes be necessary.

Consistency and Communication:

- Promote ongoing communication and collaboration among educators, specialists, parents, and students to ensure the IEP's successful implementation.

It is important to tailor the IEP to the specific needs and goals of the student, as well as to ensure alignment with state and federal special education regulations. The development and review of the IEP should involve a team approach, with input from teachers, specialists, parents, and the student, when appropriate.

WHAT IS THE PURPOSE OF MY BEHAVIOR INTERVENTION PLAN (BIP)?

Like elementary students, secondary students do not typically self-identify the need for a Behavior Intervention Plan (BIP) on their own. Instead, the decision to create a BIP is generally made by a team of educators, specialists, and parents or guardians. However, secondary students may exhibit signs or behaviors that suggest they could benefit from a BIP. It's important for adults, including teachers and school professionals, to recognize these signs and initiate the process of developing a BIP.

Here are some indications that a secondary student may need a BIP:

1. **Consistent Challenging Behaviors:** The student displays persistent and challenging behaviors that interfere with their learning, the learning of others, or the overall school environment. These behaviors may include aggression, noncompliance, disruptions, or emotional outbursts.

2. **Failure to Respond to Universal Interventions:** The student has not shown significant improvement in behavior despite the implementation of school-wide or classroom-wide behavior interventions and supports, such as a positive behavior support system or classroom management strategies.

3. **Safety Concerns:** The student's behaviors pose a safety risk to themselves, peers, or school staff. This may include physical

aggression, self-injurious behaviors, or elopement (running away).

4. **Impact on Academic Progress:** Challenging behaviors are negatively impacting the student's academic progress and their ability to access the general education curriculum. These behaviors may result in missed instruction time or disruptions during lessons.

5. **Consistency of Problem Behaviors:** The student's challenging behaviors occur consistently across different settings (e.g., classroom, cafeteria, hallways) and with different adults, suggesting that the issues are not isolated incidents.

6. **Limited Response to Consequences:** The student does not appear to respond to typical consequences or discipline strategies, such as time-outs or loss of privileges.

7. **Parent or Guardian Concerns:** Parents or guardians may express concerns about their child's behavior at school and request additional support.

8. **Data Collection:** Data collection and behavior tracking indicate a consistent pattern of problem behaviors that need to be addressed through targeted interventions.

If a secondary student exhibits one or more of these signs, it is essential for school professionals to collaborate with parents or guardians to assess the situation. This may involve conducting a Functional Behavior Assessment (FBA) to better understand the function or purpose of the problem behaviors. Based on the results of the FBA, a team can determine whether the student would benefit from a Behavior Intervention Plan (BIP).

A BIP is a comprehensive plan designed to provide targeted interventions and support to address challenging behaviors and promote positive behavior change. It should be developed with input from all relevant stakeholders, including the student's parents or guardians, and should be regularly reviewed and adjusted based on the student's progress.

WHAT IS IN THE BEHAVIOR INTERVENTION PLAN (BIP)?

A Behavior Intervention Plan (BIP) for secondary students is a specialized document designed to address and manage challenging behaviors exhibited by a middle or high school student. The BIP is developed as part of the student's Individualized Education Program (IEP) or 504 Plan, depending on the student's eligibility and needs.

Here are the standard components and elements typically included in a BIP for secondary students:

1. **Student Information:**

    - Student Name: [Student's Name]
    - Date of Birth: [Date of Birth]
    - Grade Level: [Grade]
    - School: [School Name]
    - Primary Disability or Condition: [Specify the primary disability or condition]

2. **Behavior Definitions:**

    - Clearly define the target behaviors of concern in observable and measurable terms. Describe what the behaviors look like, when and where they occur, and their frequency and duration.

3. **Functional Behavior Assessment (FBA):**

    - Summarize the results of the Functional Behavior Assessment, which helps identify the function or purpose of the problem behaviors. This understanding guides the implementation of the intervention planning.

4. **Positive Behavior Goals:**

    - Specify clear, measurable, and attainable behavior goals aimed at promoting positive behavior change. Goals should be aligned with the student's educational and social needs.

5. **Replacement Behaviors:**

    - Identify and define replacement or alternative behaviors that the student will be taught to use instead of the problem behaviors. These should serve the same function but be more appropriate.

6. **Targeted Interventions and Strategies:**

    - Outline the specific interventions and strategies that will be implemented to address the challenging behaviors. These may include:
    - Proactive strategies to prevent problem behaviors.
    - Teaching and reinforcing replacement behaviors.
    - Reinforcement and rewards for positive behavior.
    - De-escalation techniques and crisis management, if necessary.
    - Communication and social skills training.
    - Sensory support if sensory issues are a factor.

7. **Response to Behavior:**

- Describe how school staff will respond when the student exhibits the target behaviors. This may involve planned consequences, redirection, or de-escalation techniques.

8. **Data Collection and Progress Monitoring:**

    - Specify how behavior frequency, duration, and intensity data will be collected and by whom.
    - Describe the schedule for reviewing progress and adjusting interventions based on data.

9. **Crisis Intervention Plan:**

    - If the student's behavior poses a safety risk to themselves or others, outline the crisis intervention procedures, including how to maintain safety.

10. **Collaboration and Communication:**

    - Define the roles and responsibilities of school staff, parents or guardians, and any specialists involved in implementing the BIP.
    - Establish a communication plan to ensure consistency in implementing strategies across settings.

11. **Review and Revision:**

    - Specify how often the BIP will be reviewed and, if necessary, revised to assess progress and adjust as needed.

12. **Parent/Guardian Involvement:**

    - Describe how parents or guardians will be involved in implementing and reviewing the BIP. Encourage open communication and collaboration.

13. **Training and Support for Staff:**

    - Outline any training or professional development that will be provided to school staff to ensure they are equipped to implement the BIP effectively.

14. **Consistency with IEP or 504 Plan:**

    - Ensure that the BIP is consistent with other aspects of the student's IEP or 504 Plan, such as accommodations and services.

15. **Confidentiality and Privacy:**

    - Address confidentiality and privacy concerns related to sharing information about the student's BIP with appropriate school staff.

It is essential that the BIP is tailored to the specific needs of the secondary student and is developed collaboratively with input from educators, specialists, parents or guardians, and, when appropriate, the student. The plan's effectiveness should be regularly reviewed and adjusted based on the student's progress.

WHAT DO I NEED TO KNOW ABOUT MY BEHAVIOR INTERVENTION PLAN?

Secondary students typically don't self-identify the need for a Behavior Intervention Plan (BIP) on their own. Instead, the decision to create a BIP is typically made by a team of educators, specialists, and parents or guardians. However, secondary students may become aware of the need for a BIP through discussions and observations involving adults at school and home. Here are some ways a secondary student might become aware of the need for a BIP:

1. **Teacher and Staff Feedback:** Teachers and school staff may provide feedback to the students about their behavior in the classroom. If there are consistent challenges or concerns, teachers may discuss these issues with the student and explain that they are working on finding ways to help.

2. **Parent or Guardian Discussions:** Parents or guardians may have conversations with the student about their behavior at school. These discussions can include an explanation that additional support is being considered to address any challenges the student is facing.

3. **Involvement in the Process:** Depending on the student's age and level of understanding, they may be involved in the process to some extent. Older secondary students may participate in meetings where their behavior and potential interventions are discussed.

4. **Observations of Their Own Behavior:** Some students may recognize on their own that they are having difficulties with behavior or self-regulation. They may notice that their behavior is different from their peers or that they struggle with certain situations.

5. **Peer Comparisons:** Secondary students often become more aware of social dynamics and may compare their behavior to that of their peers. If they notice that they have difficulty in social situations or controlling their behavior, this may lead to self-awareness.

6. **Positive Reinforcement and Progress:** As the BIP is implemented and progress is made, the student may begin to see positive changes in their behavior and its impact on their learning and relationships. This reinforcement can contribute to their understanding of the need for the plan.

7. **Improved Self-Advocacy:** For some older secondary students, the process of developing a BIP can lead to improved self-advocacy skills. They may learn to communicate their own needs and challenges more effectively.

It is essential to approach discussions about the need for a BIP with sensitivity and support. The focus should be on helping the students understand that the plan is designed to provide them with tools and strategies to succeed academically and socially. Open and constructive communication among school professionals, parents or guardians, and the student (when appropriate) is essential for developing and implementing a BIP.

THE SIGNS THAT A SECONDARY STUDENT NEEDS AN IEP AND/OR BIP

Determining whether a secondary student needs both an Individualized Education Program (IEP) and a Behavior Intervention Plan (BIP) involves recognizing specific signs and behaviors that may indicate the need for specialized support. Here are signs that may suggest the need for an IEP and BIP for a secondary student:

Signs indicating the need for an IEP (Individualized Education Program):

1. **Academic Struggles:** The student consistently performs below grade level in one or more academic areas, such as reading, math, writing, or communication skills.

2. **Learning Disabilities:** The student shows signs of specific learning disabilities, such as dyslexia (reading difficulties), dysgraphia (writing difficulties), or dyscalculia (math difficulties).

3. **Speech or Language Delays:** Significant speech or language delays are affecting the student's ability to communicate effectively.

4. **Developmental Delays:** Signs of developmental delays in areas like motor skills, social-emotional development, or cognitive functioning may warrant consideration for an IEP.

5. **Attention and Focus Issues:** The student struggles with attention, concentration, and maintaining focus in the classroom, potentially indicating attention-deficit/hyperactivity disorder (ADHD) or other attention-related issues.

6. **Behavioral Challenges:** Problematic behaviors in the classroom that significantly disrupt learning may be a sign of underlying issues that need to be addressed through an IEP.

7. **Emotional or Behavioral Disorders:** Persistent emotional or behavioral difficulties that interfere with the student's social and emotional well-being may require specialized support.

8. **Communication and Interaction Difficulties:** Students with difficulty with social interactions, understanding social cues, or forming relationships may have autism spectrum disorder (ASD) or related conditions.

Signs Indicating the Need for a BIP (Behavior Intervention Plan):

1. **Consistent Challenging Behaviors:** The student exhibits persistent and challenging behaviors that interfere with their learning, the learning of others, or the overall school environment. These behaviors may include aggression, noncompliance, disruptions, or emotional outbursts.

2. **Failure to Respond to Universal Interventions:** The student does not show significant improvement in behavior despite the implementation of school-wide or classroom-wide behavior interventions and supports, such as a positive behavior support system or classroom management strategies.

3. **Safety Concerns:** The student's behaviors pose a safety risk to themselves, peers, or school staff. This may include physical aggression, self-injurious behaviors, or elopement (running away).

4. **Impact on Academic Progress:** Challenging behaviors significantly impede the student's ability to access and benefit from educational instruction. These behaviors may result in missed instruction time or disruptions during lessons.

5. **Consistency of Problem Behaviors:** The student's challenging behaviors occur consistently across different settings (e.g., classroom, cafeteria, hallways) and with different adults, suggesting that the issues are not isolated incidents.

6. **Limited Response to Consequences:** The student does not appear to respond to typical consequences or discipline strategies, such as time-outs or loss of privileges.

7. **Parent or Guardian Concerns:** Parents or guardians may express concerns about their child's behavior at school and request additional support.

8. **Data Collection:** Data collection and behavior tracking indicate a consistent pattern of problem behaviors that require targeted intervention strategies.

It is important to note that the decision to initiate an IEP or a BIP should involve a collaborative and multidisciplinary approach. School professionals, including teachers, specialists, behavior specialists, and administrators, should work together with parents or guardians to assess the student's needs comprehensively. The development and implementation of an IEP and BIP should be based on a thorough evaluation of the student's strengths, weaknesses, and individualized needs to ensure they receive appropriate and effective support.

EXAMPLES OF QUESTIONS TO ASK THE SECONDARY TEACHER

When considering whether a secondary student needs an Individualized Education Program (IEP), parents or guardians need open and constructive communication with the student's teacher. Asking the right questions can help gather information and insights about the student's educational needs.

Here are some examples of questions to ask the secondary teacher about the need for an IEP:

1. **What is my child's academic strengths and weaknesses in your class?**

   - Understanding your child's specific academic profile is crucial for IEP considerations.

2. **How does my child perform on standardized tests or assessments compared to their peers?**

   - Assessing standardized test scores can provide insights into your child's academic progress.

3. **Do you notice any consistent patterns of behavior or challenges my child faces in the classroom?**

- Identifying patterns of behavior or challenges can help pinpoint areas where additional support may be needed.

4. **Has my child been receiving any accommodations or modifications in the classroom?**

    - Knowing if any informal accommodations have been implemented can provide insights into potential IEP accommodations.

5. **Are there any specific challenges my child faces during transitions between classes or activities?**

    - Transition challenges can indicate potential executive function or organizational difficulties.

6. **Does my child have difficulty with assignments, homework, or classwork completion?**

    - Understanding homework and assignment completion issues can help tailor IEP goals.

7. **Has there been a noticeable change in my child's behavior or academic performance over time?**

    - Changes in behavior or performance may suggest underlying issues that need attention.

8. **Have you observed any difficulties with my child's social interactions or peer relationships?**

- Social challenges can be an important consideration, especially for students with autism spectrum disorders or social-emotional difficulties.

9. **What specific accommodations or modifications do you believe would benefit my child's learning experience?**

   - The teacher's input can guide discussions about potential IEP accommodations.

10. **Do you believe my child would benefit from additional support services or specialized instruction?**

    - This question directly addresses the need for an IEP and invites the teacher's input.

11. **What strategies have you used to address my child's challenges, and how effective have they been?**

    - Understanding the effectiveness of existing strategies can help guide the development of the IEP.

12. **Can we schedule a meeting with the school's special education team to discuss my child's needs and potential eligibility for an IEP?**

    - Requesting a meeting with the school's special education team is an important step in the IEP evaluation process.

Remember that the teacher's input is valuable. Still, the decision to pursue an IEP should be based on a collaborative process involving educators, specialists, parents or guardians, and, when appropriate, the student. Suppose there are concerns about a student's educational needs. In that case, it may be appropriate to request an evaluation by the school district's special education team to determine eligibility for special education services, including the development of an IEP.

EXAMPLES OF QUESTIONS TO ASK THE SECONDARY TEACHER ABOUT NEEDING A 504 SERVICE PLAN

When considering whether a secondary student may need a 504 Plan, it is essential for parents or guardians to have open and constructive communication with the student's teacher. A 504 Plan provides accommodations and support to students with disabilities who do not qualify for special education services under an Individualized Education Program (IEP).

Here are some examples of questions to ask the secondary teacher about the need for a 504 Plan:

1. **What specific challenges or barriers has my child been facing in your class?**

    - Understanding the specific challenges your child is experiencing is essential for determining the need for accommodations.

2. **Have you noticed any consistent patterns of behavior or difficulties that may be related to a disability?**

    - Identifying patterns of behavior or challenges can help pinpoint areas where accommodations may be beneficial.

3. **Are there any documented medical or educational diagnoses that may impact my child's ability to access and benefit from education?**

    - If your child has a diagnosed condition or medical issue, it's important to discuss how it affects their educational experience.

4. **Has my child been receiving any accommodations or support in the classroom?**

    - Knowing if any informal accommodations have been implemented can provide insights into potential 504 Plan accommodations.

5. **Do you think my child may benefit from formal accommodations to ensure equal access to educational opportunities?**

    - This question directly addresses the need for a 504 Plan and invites the teacher's input.

6. **Are there any specific accommodations or strategies that you believe would be helpful for my child?**

    - The teacher's suggestions for accommodations can guide discussions with the school's 504 Plan coordinator.

7. **How do my child's challenges impact their academic performance and overall school experience?**

- Understanding the impact of the challenges on your child's education is essential for making informed decisions.

8. **Is it possible to schedule a meeting with the school's 504 Plan coordinator to discuss my child's needs and potential accommodations?**

    - Requesting a meeting with the 504 Plan coordinator is a crucial step in the process of developing a 504 Plan.

9. **Are there any relevant assessments or documentation that can support the need for a 504 Plan?**

    - In some cases, assessments or documentation may be necessary to establish the need for accommodations.

10. **What can I do at home to support my child's learning and address their challenges?**

    - The teacher may have suggestions for how you can support your child's education outside of school.

11. **Can you provide examples of how specific accommodations might help my child succeed in your class?**

    - Concrete examples of accommodations can help you understand their potential impact.

12. **Can I sue the teacher and the school if my child's 504 service plan is not being implemented?**

- Yes, you will contact the Office of Civil Rights office to file a complaint, and to pursue a due process hiring, you can hire an attorney at your expense.

Remember that the teacher's input is valuable. Still, the decision to pursue a 504 Plan should be based on a collaborative process involving educators, specialists, parents or guardians, and the school's 504 coordinator. If there is agreement that a 504 Plan is necessary, the process will typically include an evaluation to determine eligibility and the specific accommodations that will be included in the plan.

FIVE WAYS TO HELP K–12 STUDENTS ADVOCATE FOR THEMSELVES

1. *Encourage students to ask questions (and acknowledge challenging content)*

Asking questions is hard for students because they often don't want to call attention to themselves or the fact that they don't understand something. When I was teaching, I found that students were more likely to come to me at the end of class to ask questions, so I made sure to leave time for students to have that one-on-one opportunity.

Another way to help students speak up is to ask pointed questions such as, "What's still confusing?" or, "What part should I explain again?" I've taken the stigma out of needing clarification because I've already assumed that the content is challenging. This allows students to speak up without feeling like they are the only ones still puzzled.

2. *Teach students about metacognition*

A meaningful way to model self-advocacy is to teach students how to think about their thinking. I used to tell a lot of stories and explain my own thought processes to encourage my students to do the same. Part of knowing what we need is self-assessing and determining where we have challenges. Teachers can lead students to this reflection, and so can parents. Asking students to reflect on a lesson in an explicit way leads them to identify how they learn best. Plus, once they know when and why they reach a point of frustration, they will then be equipped to determine when it's time to ask for help.

3. *Help students reflect on their strengths and weaknesses*

As adults, we are often self-aware enough to say, "I don't do well in those types of situations. I prefer this other kind of situation." Young students are not as self-aware, but through guided metacognition, they can reflect on their strengths and weaknesses and know when a challenge or roadblock is ahead. Students with learning disabilities are taught to think this way, but it doesn't always mean they will advocate for themselves when they see a roadblock ahead. As they cope with difficult learning situations, they may shut down. In those moments, it is helpful for students to practice identifying roadblocks and problem-solving—with the help of a trusted adult—how to overcome them.

4. *Offer resources and options*

I conducted a number of conferences with parents and their students, in which my colleagues and I encouraged struggling high schoolers to ask for help or stay after school when they needed additional support. And so many times, students didn't do it. That's why students of every age need choices. Asking for help from a teacher is often the best option but not always the most attractive. Logging in to an anonymous tutoring service outside of the school walls might be easier. Starting a study group with good friends might be more enticing. Talking to students about their options and when they can use each of these resources is another way to strengthen the connection between needing help and advocating for oneself.

5. *Model a growth mindset*

The most important thing students can learn is that they can learn. A growth mindset sets the stage for the fact that learning is not impossible. There is always a solution or support that can help students get through and beyond a difficult situation. Students need to know how to advocate for themselves and learn self-determination at the same time. As they do, they are likely to find that the most frustrating setbacks often provide the greatest—and most memorable—opportunities for growth. (Dietzman, 2023)

APPENDIX

Special Education is full of terms people constantly use in writing and conversation, and it is important to know what they mean. This handy reference to special education terminology helps you quickly connect with the meaning of pivotal words and phrases in the field.

INDEX TO THE TERMS AND MEANING

- Point of Reference: IDEA
- Child Find
- A child with a disability
- FAPE | Free appropriate public education
- IDEA | Individuals with Disabilities Education Act
- IEP | Individualized Education Program
- LRE | Least Restrictive Environment
- Related services
- Special education
- Supplementary aids and services
- Transition services
- TA&D | Technical Assistance and Dissemination

Point of Reference: IDEA

It is extremely important to understand that the terms you will likely hear in special education come from our nation's special education law, the IDEA (Individuals with Disabilities Education Act). We frequently refer to this law on our website and in our publications because it guides how special education and related services are provided to children with disabilities in the United States. States develop their own special education policies and procedures based on what IDEA requires. They are allowed to go beyond what IDEA requires–and frequently do, because the law leaves a great many things to state and local discretion–but they are not permitted to have policies or procedures inconsistent with IDEA's provisions.

This being the case, the starting point of special education terms and what they mean is always IDEA's definitions. Your state's definition of a term is also important to consider because it will influence how the term is being used in your area, especially if the state definition is not the same as IDEA's.

CHILD FIND is the affirmative, ongoing obligation of local education agencies (LEAs) to identify, locate, and evaluate all children with disabilities residing within their jurisdictions who need special education and related services.

The LEA's responsibility for child find is for all children with disabilities ages 0-21. The LEA is responsible for identifying, locating, and evaluating all children with disabilities who need special education and related services. The LEA's responsibility for free appropriate public education (FAPE) is for children with disabilities ages 3-21. Services must be available to ALL eligible students by their third birthday.

LEAs must have established outreach activities designed to locate children with disabilities who reside within the jurisdiction of the LEA, including children who are homeless or wards of the state, incarcerated, or in private schools (including home schools). The LEA's public awareness campaign should target a wide variety of people who may work with the LEA's students.

Public awareness may include posters placed on campuses and district administration buildings.

Child with a Disability

IDEA defines this very important term as follows:

§300.8 Child with a disability

(a) **General**. (1) Child with a disability means a child evaluated in accordance with §§300.304 through 300.311 as having an intellectual disability, a hearing impairment (including deafness), a speech or language impairment, a visual impairment (including blindness), a serious emotional disturbance (referred to in this part as "emotional disturbance"), an orthopedic impairment, autism, traumatic brain injury, another health impairment, a specific learning disability, deaf-blindness, or multiple disabilities, and who, by reason thereof, needs special education and related services.

(2)(i) Subject to paragraph (a)(2)(ii) of this section, if it is determined, through an appropriate evaluation under §§300.304 through 300.311, that a child has one of the disabilities identified in paragraph (a)(1) of this section, but only needs a related service and not special education, the child is not a child with a disability under this part.

(ii) If consistent with §300.39(a)(2), the related service required by the child is considered special education rather than a related service under State standards, the child would be determined to be a child with a disability under paragraph (a)(1) of this section.

(b) Children aged three through nine experiencing developmental delays. A child with a disability for children aged three through nine (or any subset of that age range, including ages three through five) may, subject to the conditions described in §300.111(b), include a child—

1) Who is experiencing developmental delays, as defined by the State and as measured by appropriate diagnostic instruments and procedures, in one or more of the following areas: Physical development, cognitive development, communication development, social or emotional development, or adaptive development; and

2) Who, by reason thereof, needs special education and related services?

Editor's note: We've included the text of §300.111(b), mentioned above and very relevant to "Developmental Delay," at the very end of this definition of "child with a disability."

(c) **Definitions of disability terms**. The terms used in this definition of a child with a disability are defined as follows:

1) *Autism* means a developmental disability significantly affecting verbal and nonverbal communication and social interaction, generally evident before age three, that adversely affects a child's educational performance. Other characteristics often associated with autism are engagement

in repetitive activities and stereotyped movements, resistance to environmental change or change in daily routines, and unusual responses to sensory experiences.

(ii) Autism does not apply if a child's educational performance is adversely affected primarily because the child has an emotional disturbance, as defined in paragraph (c)(4) of this section.

(iii) A child who manifests the characteristics of autism after age three could be identified as having autism if the criteria in paragraph (c)(1)(i) of this section are satisfied.

2) *Deaf-blindness* means concomitant hearing and visual impairments, the combination of which causes such severe communication and other developmental and educational needs that they cannot be accommodated in special education programs solely for children with deafness or children with blindness.

3) *Deafness* means a hearing impairment that is so severe that the child is impaired in processing linguistic information through hearing, with or without amplification, that adversely affects a child's educational performance.

4) *Emotional disturbance* means a condition exhibiting one or more of the following characteristics over a long period of time and to a marked degree that adversely affects a child's educational performance:

A. An inability to learn that cannot be explained by intellectual, sensory, or health factors.
B. An inability to build or maintain satisfactory interpersonal relationships with peers and teachers.
C. Inappropriate types of behavior or feelings under normal circumstances.

D. A general pervasive mood of unhappiness or depression.
E. A tendency to develop physical symptoms or fears associated with personal or school problems.
(ii) Emotional disturbance includes schizophrenia. The term does not apply to children who are socially maladjusted unless it is determined that they have an emotional disturbance under paragraph (c)(4) (i) of this section.

5) *Hearing impairment* means an impairment in hearing, whether permanent or fluctuating, that adversely affects a child's educational performance, but that is not included under the definition of deafness in this section.

6) *Intellectual disability*** means significantly subaverage general intellectual functioning, existing concurrently with deficits in adaptive behavior and manifested during the developmental period, that adversely affects a child's educational performance.

7) *Multiple disabilities* mean concomitant impairments (such as intellectual disability-blindness or intellectual disability-orthopedic impairment), the combination of which causes such severe educational needs that they cannot be accommodated in special education programs solely for one of the impairments. Multiple disabilities do not include deaf-blindness.

8) *Orthopedic impairment* means a severe orthopedic impairment that adversely affects a child's educational performance. The term includes impairments caused by a congenital anomaly, impairments caused by disease (e.g., poliomyelitis, bone tuberculosis), and impairments from other causes (e.g.,

cerebral palsy, amputations, and fractures or burns that cause contractures).

9) *Other health impairment* means having limited strength, vitality, or alertness, including a heightened alertness to environmental stimuli, that results in limited alertness with respect to the educational environment, that—
   (i) Is due to chronic or acute health problems such as asthma, attention deficit disorder or attention deficit hyperactivity disorder, diabetes, epilepsy, a heart condition, hemophilia, lead poisoning, leukemia, nephritis, rheumatic fever, sickle cell anemia, and Tourette syndrome; and
   (ii) Adversely affects a child's educational performance.

10) *Specific learning disability*—(i) *General.* A specific learning disability means a disorder in one or more of the basic psychological processes involved in understanding or in using language, spoken or written, that may manifest itself in the imperfect ability to listen, think, speak, read, write, spell, or to do mathematical calculations, including conditions such as perceptual disabilities, brain injury, minimal brain dysfunction, dyslexia, and developmental aphasia.
   (ii) *Disorders not included.* A specific learning disability does not include learning problems that are primarily the result of visual, hearing, or motor disabilities, intellectual disability, emotional disturbance, or environmental, cultural, or economic disadvantage.

11) *Speech or language impairment* means a communication disorder, such as stuttering, impaired articulation, a language impairment, or a voice impairment, that adversely affects a child's educational performance.

12) *Traumatic brain injury* means an acquired injury to the brain caused by an external physical force, resulting in total or partial functional disability, psychosocial impairment, or both, that adversely affects a child's educational performance. Traumatic brain injury applies to open or closed head injuries resulting in impairments in one or more areas, such as cognition, language, memory, attention, reasoning; abstract thinking, judgment; problem-solving, sensory, perceptual, and motor abilities, psychosocial behavior, physical functions; information processing; and speech. Traumatic brain injury does not apply to brain injuries that are congenital or degenerative or to brain injuries induced by birth trauma.

13) *Visual impairment*, including blindness, means an impairment in vision that, even with correction, adversely affects a child's educational performance. The term includes both partial sight and blindness.

Here are the provisions at §300.111(b) Relevant to "Developmental Delay"

(b) *Use of the term developmental delay.* The following provisions apply with respect to implementing the child find requirements of this section:

1) A State that adopts a definition of developmental delay under §300.8(b) determines whether the term applies to children aged three through nine or to a subset of that age range (e.g., ages three through five).
2) A State may not require an LEA to adopt and use the term developmental delay for any children within its jurisdiction.

3) If an LEA uses the term developmental delay for children described in §300.8(b), the LEA must conform to both the State's definition of that term and to the age range that the State has adopted.
4) If a State does not adopt the term developmental delay, an LEA may not independently use that term to establish a child's eligibility under this part.

Editor's note, February 2011:
Prior to October 2010, IDEA used the term "mental retardation." In October 2010, President Obama signed Rosa's Law into law. Rosa's Law changed the term to be used in the future to "intellectual disability." The definition of the term itself did not change, only the term to be used (now "intellectual disability").

FAPE | Free Appropriate Public Education
IDEA defines this term (also referred to as FAPE for short) as follows:
§300.17 Free appropriate public education

Free appropriate public education or *FAPE* means special education and related services that—

(a) Are provided at public expense, under public supervision and direction, and without charge;
(b) Meet the standards of the SEA, including the requirements of this part;
(c) Include an appropriate preschool, elementary school, or secondary school education in the State involved; and

(d) Are provided in conformity with an individualized education program (IEP) that meets the requirements of §§300.320 through 300.324.

IDEA

IDEA is an acronym for the **Individuals with Disabilities Education Act**, our nation's special education law. IDEA was first passed in 1975. It was called the Education for All Handicapped Children's Act. Every few years, the law has been revised (a process called *reauthorization*).

The most current version of IDEA is **Public Law 108-446**, passed in 2004 and called the "Individuals with Disabilities Education Improvement Act of 2004." It's still most commonly referred to as IDEA or IDEA 2004 (to distinguish it from other reauthorizations). **Final regulations for IDEA 2004** were published in 2006.

IEP | Individualized Education Program (IEP)

IDEA defines this term as follows:

§300.22 Individualized Education Program

Individualized education program or *IEP* means a written statement for a child with a disability that is developed, reviewed, and revised in accordance with §§300.320 through 300.324.

In addition to this brief definition of the term at §300.22, IDEA includes a much longer, much more useful description at §300.320.

§300.320 Definition of individualized education program.

(a) **General**. As used in this part, the term individualized education program or IEP means a written statement for each child with a disability that is developed, reviewed, and revised in a meeting in accordance with §§300.320 through 300.324, and that must include—

1) A statement of the child's present levels of academic achievement and functional performance, including—

(i) How the child's disability affects the child's involvement and progress in the general education curriculum (i.e., the same curriculum as for nondisabled children); or

(ii) For preschool children, as appropriate, how the disability affects the child's participation in appropriate activities;

2) A statement of measurable annual goals, including academic and functional goals designed to—

A. Meet the child's needs that result from the child's disability to enable the child to be involved in and make progress in the general education curriculum and

B. Meet each of the child's other educational needs that result from the child's disability;

(ii) For children with disabilities who take alternate assessments aligned to alternate achievement standards, a description of benchmarks or short-term objectives;

(3) A description of—

(i) How the child's progress toward meeting the annual goals described in paragraph (2) of this section will be measured; and

(ii) When periodic reports on the progress the child is making toward meeting the annual goals (such as through the use of quarterly or other periodic reports, concurrent with the issuance of report cards) will be provided;

(4) A statement of the special education and related services and supplementary aids and services, based on peer-reviewed research to the extent practicable, to be

provided to the child or on behalf of the child, and a statement of the program modifications or supports for school personnel that will be provided to enable the child—

(i) To advance appropriately toward attaining the annual goals;

(ii) To be involved in and make progress in the general education curriculum in accordance with paragraph (a)(1) of this section, and to participate in extracurricular and other nonacademic activities; and

(iii) To be educated and participate with other children with disabilities and nondisabled children in the activities described in this section;

3) An explanation of the extent, if any, to which the child will not participate with nondisabled children in the regular class and the activities described in paragraph (a)(4) of this section;

4) A statement of any individual appropriate accommodations that are necessary to measure the academic achievement and functional performance of the child on State and districtwide assessments consistent with §612(a) (16) of the Act; and

(ii) If the IEP Team determines that the child must take an alternate assessment instead of a particular regular State or districtwide assessment of student achievement, a statement of why—

(A) The child cannot participate in the regular assessment; and

(B) The particular alternate assessment selected is appropriate for the child and

The projected date for the beginning of the services and modifications described in paragraph (a)(4) of this section and the anticipated frequency, location, and duration of those services and modifications.

(b) **Transition services**. Beginning not later than the first IEP to be in effect when the child turns 16 or younger if determined appropriate by the IEP Team, and updated annually, thereafter, the IEP must include—

(1) Appropriate measurable postsecondary goals based upon age-appropriate transition assessments related to training, education, employment, and, where appropriate, independent living skills; and

(2) The transition services (including courses of study) needed to assist the child in reaching those goals.

(c) **Transfer of rights at the age of majority**. Beginning not later than one year before the child reaches the age of majority under State law, the IEP must include a statement that the child has been informed of the child's rights under Part B of the Act, if any, that will transfer to the child on reaching the age of majority under §300.520.

(d) **Construction**. Nothing in this section shall be construed to require—

(1) That additional information be included in a child's IEP beyond what is explicitly required in section 614 of the Act; or

(2) The IEP Team should include information under one component of a child's IEP that is already contained under another IEP.

LRE | Least Restrictive Environment

IDEA's provisions with respect to LRE are not a "definition" per se, but they are nonetheless very important to know. These provisions appear in the final Part B regulations at §§300.114 through 300.120 as part of IDEA's provisions addressing "State Eligibility." The conceptual core of IDEA's LRE provisions is at §300.114, cited below.

§300.114 LRE requirements.

(a) *General.* (1) Except as provided in §300.324(d)(2) (regarding children with disabilities in adult prisons), the State must have in effect policies and procedures to ensure that public agencies in the State meet the LRE requirements of this section and §§ 300.115 through 300.120.

(2) Each public agency must ensure that—

(i) To the maximum extent appropriate, children with disabilities, including children in public or private institutions or other care facilities, are educated with children who are nondisabled; and

(ii) Special classes, separate schooling, or other removal of children with disabilities from the regular educational environment occurs only if the nature or severity of the disability is such that education in regular classes with the use of supplementary aids and services cannot be achieved satisfactorily.

(b) *Additional requirement*—State funding mechanism— (1) *General.* (i) A State funding mechanism must not result in placements that violate the requirements of paragraph (a) of this section; and

(ii) A State must not use a funding mechanism by which the State distributes funds on the basis of the type of setting in which a child is served that will result in the failure to provide a child with a disability FAPE according to the unique needs of the child, as described in the child's IEP.

(2) *Assurance.* If the State does not have policies and procedures to ensure compliance with paragraph (b)(1) of this section, the State must provide the Secretary an assurance that the State will revise the funding mechanism as soon as feasible to ensure that the mechanism does not result in placements that violate that paragraph.

Related services

IDEA defines this term as follows:

§300.34 Related services.

(a) *General.* Related services mean transportation and such developmental, corrective, and other supportive services as are required to assist a child with a disability to benefit from special education, and include speech-language pathology and audiology services, interpreting services, psychological services, physical and occupational therapy, recreation, including therapeutic recreation, early identification and assessment of disabilities in children, counseling services, including rehabilitation counseling, orientation, and mobility services, and medical services for diagnostic or evaluation purposes. Related services also include school health services and school nurse services, social work services in schools, and parent counseling and training.

(b) *Exception*: services that apply to children with surgically implanted devices, including cochlear implants.

(1) Related services do not include a medical device that is surgically implanted, the optimization of that device's functioning (e.g., mapping), maintenance of that device, or the replacement of that device.

(2) Nothing in paragraph (b)(1) of this section—

(i) Limits the right of a child with a surgically implanted device (e.g., cochlear implant) to receive related services (as listed in paragraph (a) of this section) that are determined by the IEP Team to be necessary for the child to receive FAPE.

(ii) Limits the responsibility of a public agency to appropriately monitor and maintain medical devices that are needed to maintain the health and safety of the child, including breathing, nutrition, or operation of other bodily functions, while the child is transported to and from school or is at school; or

(iii) Prevents the routine checking of an external component of a surgically implanted device to ensure it functions properly, as required in §300.113(b).

(c) *Individual related services terms defined.* The terms used in this definition are defined as follows:

(1) **Audiology** includes—

(i) Identification of children with hearing loss;

(ii) Determination of the range, nature, and degree of hearing loss, including referral for medical or other professional attention for the habilitation of hearing;

(iii) Provision of habilitative activities, such as language habilitation, auditory training, speech reading (lip-reading), hearing evaluation, and speech conservation;

(iv) Creation and administration of programs for prevention of hearing loss;

(v) Counseling and guidance of children, parents, and teachers regarding hearing loss; and

(vi) Determination of children's needs for group and individual amplification, selecting and fitting an appropriate aid, and evaluating the effectiveness of amplification.

(2) *Counseling services* are provided by qualified social workers, psychologists, guidance counselors, or other qualified personnel.

(3) **Early identification and assessment of disabilities in children** means implementing a formal plan for identifying a disability as early as possible in a child's life.

(4) **Interpreting services** include—

(i) The following, when used with respect to children who are deaf or hard of hearing: Oral transliteration services, cued language transliteration services, sign language transliteration and interpreting services, and transcription services, such as communication access real-time translation (CART), C-Print, and TypeWell; and

(ii) Special interpreting services for children who are deaf-blind.

(5) **Medical services** mean services provided by a licensed physician to determine a child's medically related disability that results in the child's need for special education and related services.

(6) **Occupational therapy—**

(i) Means services provided by a qualified occupational therapist; and

(ii) Includes—

(A) Improving, developing, or restoring functions impaired or lost through illness, injury, or deprivation;

(B) Improving the ability to perform tasks for independent functioning if functions are impaired or lost; and

(C) Preventing, through early intervention, initial or further impairment or loss of function.

(7) **Orientation and mobility services—**

(i) Means services provided to blind or visually impaired children by qualified personnel to enable those students to attain systematic orientation to and safe movement within their environments in school, home, and community; and

(ii) Includes teaching children the following, as appropriate:

(A) Spatial and environmental concepts and use of information received by the senses (such as sound, temperature, and vibrations) to establish, maintain, or regain orientation and line of travel (e.g., using sound at a traffic light to cross the street);

(B) To use the long cane or a service animal to supplement visual travel skills or as a tool for safely negotiating the environment for children with no available travel vision;

(C) To understand and use remaining vision and distance low vision aids; and

(D) Other concepts, techniques, and tools.

(8)(i) **Parent counseling and training** means assisting parents in understanding the special needs of their child;

(ii) Providing parents with information about child development; and

(iii) Helping parents acquire the necessary skills that will allow them to support the implementation of their child's IEP or IFSP.

(9) **Physical therapy** means services provided by a qualified physical therapist.

(10) **Psychological services** include—

(i) Administering psychological and educational tests and other assessment procedures;

(ii) Interpreting assessment results;

(iii) Obtaining, integrating, and interpreting information about child behavior and conditions relating to learning;

(iv) Consulting with other staff members in planning school programs to meet the special educational needs of children as indicated by psychological tests, interviews, direct observation, and behavioral evaluations;

(v) Planning and managing a program of psychological services, including psychological counseling for children and parents; and

(vi) Assisting in developing positive behavioral intervention strategies.

(11) **Recreation** includes—

(i) Assessment of leisure function;

(ii) Therapeutic recreation services;

(iii) Recreation programs in schools and community agencies; and

(iv) Leisure education.

(12) **Rehabilitation counseling services** means services provided by qualified personnel in individual or group sessions that focus specifically on career development, employment preparation, achieving independence, and integration in the workplace and community of a student with a disability. The term also includes vocational rehabilitation services provided to a student with a

disability by vocational rehabilitation programs funded under the Rehabilitation Act of 1973, as amended, 29 U.S.C. 701 et seq.

(13) **School health services and school nurse service***s* are health services that are designed to enable a child with a disability to receive FAPE as described in the child's IEP. School nurse services are services provided by a qualified school nurse. School health services may be provided by either a qualified school nurse or another qualified person.

(14) **Social work services in schools** include—

(i) Preparing a social or developmental history of a child with a disability;

(ii) Group and individual counseling with the child and family;

(iii) Working in partnership with parents and others on those problems in a child's living situation (home, school, and community) that affect the child's adjustment in school;

(iv) Mobilizing school and community resources to enable the child to learn as effectively as possible in his or her educational program; and

(v) Assisting in developing positive behavioral intervention strategies.

(15) **Speech-language pathology service***s* include—

(i) Identification of children with speech or language impairments;

(ii) Diagnosis and appraisal of specific speech or language impairments;

(iii) Referral for medical or other professional attention necessary for the habilitation of speech or language impairments;

(iv) Provision of speech and language services for the habilitation or prevention of communicative impairments; and

(v) Counseling and guidance of parents, children, and teachers regarding speech and language impairments.

(16) **Transportation** includes—

(i) Travel to and from school and between schools;

(ii) Travel in and around school buildings; and

(iii) Specialized equipment (such as special or adapted buses, lifts, and ramps), if required, to provide special transportation for a child with a disability.

Special Education

IDEA defines "special education" as follows:

§300.39 Special education.

(a) *General.* (1) Special education means specially designed instruction, at no cost to the parents, to meet the unique needs of a child with a disability, including—

(i) Instruction conducted in the classroom, in the home, in hospitals and institutions, and in other settings; and

(ii) Instruction in physical education.

(2) Special education includes each of the following if the services otherwise meet the requirements of paragraph (a)(1) of this section—

(i) Speech-language pathology services, or any other related service, if the service is considered special education rather than a related service under State standards;

(ii) Travel training; and

(iii) Vocational education.

(b) *Individual special education terms defined.* The terms in this definition are defined as follows:

(1) **At no cost** means that all specially-designed instruction is provided without charge but does not preclude incidental fees normally charged to nondisabled students or their parents as a part of the regular education program.

(2) *Physical education* means—

(i) The development of—

(A) Physical and motor fitness;

(B) Fundamental motor skills and patterns; and

(C) Skills in aquatics, dance, and individual and group games and sports (including intramural and lifetime sports); and

(ii) Includes special physical education, adapted physical education, movement education, and motor development.

(3) **Specially designed instruction** means adapting, as appropriate to the needs of an eligible child under this part, the content, methodology, or delivery of instruction—

(i) To address the unique needs of the child that result from the child's disability; and

(ii) To ensure access of the child to the general curriculum so that the child can meet the educational standards within the jurisdiction of the public agency that apply to all children.

(4) **Travel training** means providing instruction, as appropriate, to children with significant cognitive disabilities and any other children with disabilities who require this instruction to enable them to—

(i) Develop an awareness of the environment in which they live; and

(ii) Learn the skills necessary to move effectively and safely from place to place within that environment (e.g., in school, in the home, at work, and in the community).

(5) **Vocational education** means organized educational programs directly related to the preparation of individuals for paid or unpaid employment or additional preparation for a career not requiring a baccalaureate or advanced degree.

Supplementary Aids and Services

IDEA defines "supplementary aids and services" as follows:

§300.42 Supplementary aids and services.

Supplementary aids and services mean aids, services, and other supports that are provided in regular education classes, other education-related settings, and in extracurricular and nonacademic settings to enable children with disabilities to be educated with nondisabled children to the maximum extent appropriate in accordance with §§300.114 through 300.116.

Transition Services

IDEA defines "transition services" as follows:

§300.43 Transition services.

(a) *Transition services* means a coordinated set of activities for a child with a disability that—

(1) Is designed to be within a results-oriented process that is focused on improving the academic and functional achievement of the child with a disability to facilitate the child's movement from school to post-school activities, including postsecondary education, vocational education, integrated employment (including supported employment), continuing and adult education, adult services, independent living, or community participation;

(2) Is based on the individual child's needs, considering the child's strengths, preferences, and interests, and includes—

(i) Instruction;

(ii) Related services;

(iii) Community experiences;

(iv) The development of employment and other post-school adult living objectives; and

(v) If appropriate, acquisition of daily living skills and provision of a functional vocational evaluation.

(b) Transition services for children with disabilities may be special education if provided as specially designed instruction or a related service if required to assist a child with a disability to benefit from special education.

TA&D | Technical Assistance and Dissemination Network

Editor's note: IDEA's provisions with respect to the Technical Assistance and Dissemination (TA&D) network of OSEP do not contain a "definition" of TA&D but, rather, authorize the Secretary of Education to fund projects intended to improve the education of children with disabilities. In Section 663 of the statute (Public Law 108-446), the following authorization
appears:

"(e) *Linking States to Information Sources.*—In carrying out this section, the Secretary shall support projects that link States to technical assistance resources, including special education and general education resources, and shall make research and related products available through libraries, electronic networks, parent training projects, and other information sources, including through the activities of the National Center for Education Evaluation and Regional Assistance established under part D of the Education Sciences Reform Act of 2002."

(Lowry, 2023)

At a Glance:
Free and Appropriate Public Education (FAPE)

FAPE stands for free and appropriate public education. It's one of the most important legal terms for you to know. Learn the details behind this powerful acronym.

F

Free means that all eligible students with disabilities will be educated at public expense. There is no cost to you, the parent. You do, however, have to pay the same incidental fees (such as membership fees for clubs) as for general education students.

A

Appropriate means that your child with a disability is entitled to an education that is appropriate for her. It will be tailored and planned to meet her needs as stated in her Individualized Education Program (IEP).

P

Public refers to the public school system. Children with disabilities, whatever the nature or severity of their disabilities, have the right to be educated under public supervision. (Many children will be educated in the public school. In some cases, they might be educated in a private school.)

E

Education must be provided to every eligible school-age child with a disability. If this describes your child, FAPE ensures that she'll receive a public education that includes the services outlined in her Individualized Education Program (IEP). The education should prepare your child for the future—further education, employment and independent living.

Understood

for learning & attention issues

For more tips and resources, go to **understood.org**

Copyright © 2014 Understood.org USA LLC

300.101 Free appropriate public education (FAPE).

(a) General. A free, appropriate public education must be available to all children residing in the State between the ages of 3 and 21, inclusive, including children with disabilities who have been suspended or expelled from school, as provided for in §300.530 (d).

(b) FAPE for children beginning at age 3.

(1) Each State must ensure that—

(i) The obligation to make FAPE available to each eligible child residing in the State begins no later than the child's third birthday; and
(ii) An IEP or an IFSP is in effect for the child by that date, in accordance with §300.323(b).

(2) If a child's third birthday occurs during the summer, the child's IEP Team shall determine the date when services under the IEP or IFSP will begin.

(c) Children advancing from grade to grade.

(1) Each State must ensure that FAPE is available to any individual child with a disability who needs special education and related services, even though the child has not failed or been retained in a course or grade and is advancing from grade to grade.
(2) The determination that a child described in paragraph (a) of this section is eligible under this part must be made on an individual basis by the group responsible within the child's LEA for making eligibility determinations. (IDEA, 2023)

(IDEA, 2023)

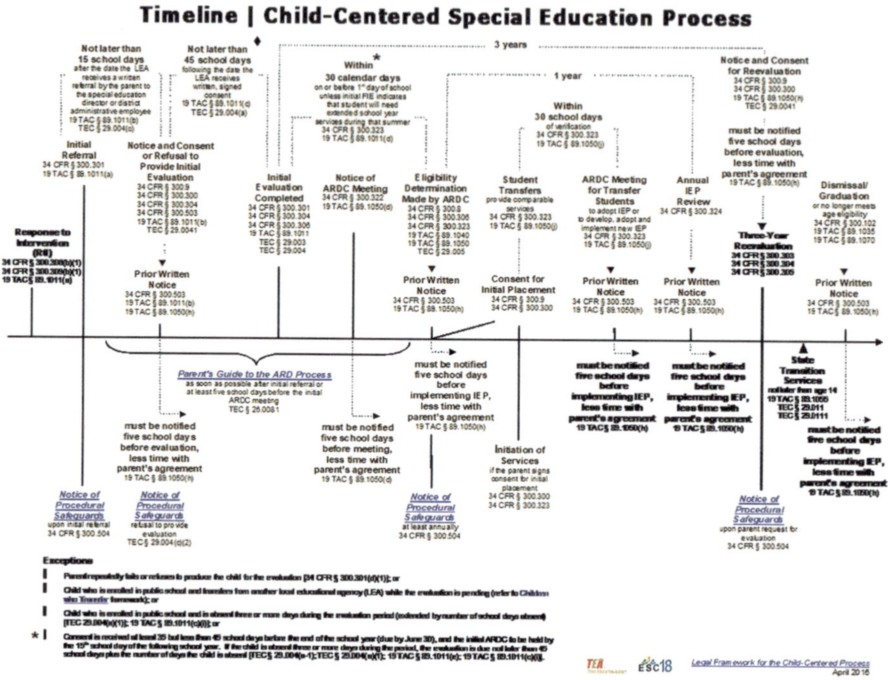
Timeline | Child-Centered Special Education Process
3 years
1 year
Not later than 15 school days
Not later than 45 school days
Within 30 calendar days
Within 30 school days
Notice and Consent for Reevaluation
Initial Referral
Notice and Consent or Refusal to Provide Initial Evaluation
Initial Evaluation Completed
Notice of ARDC Meeting
Eligibility Determination Made by ARDC
Student Transfers
ARDC Meeting for Transfer Students
Annual IEP Review
must be notified five school days before evaluation, less time with parent's agreement
Dismissal/ Graduation
Response to Intervention (RtI)
Prior Written Notice
Consent for Initial Placement
Three-Year Reevaluation
Parent's Guide to the ARD Process
must be notified five school days before implementing IEP, less time with parent's agreement
must be notified five school days before meeting, less time with parent's agreement
State Transition Services
Initiation of Services
Notice of Procedural Safeguards
Exceptions
Legal Framework for the Child-Centered Process
April 2016

APPENDIX 1

Name: ______________________ Date: ____________________

Emotions

Look at the pictures and circle the correct words

	EXCITED WORRIED		JOYFUL SATISFIED
	TIRED AMUSED		PROUD IRRITATED
	CONFUSED GRATEFUL		SURPRISED HAPPY
	HUNGRY ANGRY		MOODY TIRED
	SLEEPY FRUSTRATED		FED UP SURPRISED

APPENDIX 2

Permission to make copies

WEEKLY SCHEDULE

Monday

Tuesday

Wednesday

Thursday

Friday

Notes

APPENDIX 3

Exploring my emotions

Can you name your emotions?

Write the names of these emotions.

________ ________ ________ ________ ________

________ ________ ________ ________ ________

Can you recognize your emotions?

Read and answer about you.

How do you feel when it is your birthday? ________________

How do you feel when you fail a test? ________________

How do you feel when it rains? ________________

How do you feel when someone hugs you? ________________

How do you feel when you have a nightmare? ________________

Can you express and explain your emotions?

Think how you feel at this moment and draw it. Then explain why you feel this way.

____

____

____

____

Permission to make copies

APPENDIX 4

IEP Accommodation and Modification Checklist

Student	None	Preferential Seating	Small Group Instruction Testing	Individual Instruction Testing	Extra Time Tests/ Assignment	Modify/ Repeat/ Model Directions	Allow Breaks	Test Read Aloud	Modify Assignments as Needed	Assistive Technology - List	Other - List

Note: Place an "X" next to a student's name if the student receives the accommodation listed in the column.

Permission to make copies

APPENDIX 5

ASSIGNMENT LOG for ______________________________

NAME ______________________________

CLASS ______________________________

First	Last	Date	Time	Comments

APPENDIX 6

Daily Class Participation and Communication

Teacher ______________________________

Student ______________________________

Parent ______________________________

Date		Initials

Permission to make copies

Parent to Parent Connection Advocacy, Inc.'s mission is to enhance the knowledge of parents with school-aged children. To ensure and encourage maximum involvement by parents and the community. We strive to educate our community by distributing resources focused on special needs and children with disabilities in an efficient and accountable manner.

For more information about the services that Parent-to-Parent Connection Advocacy, Inc., (PPCA) provides to parents or if you need an advocate, see below and contact us today:

- Increase understanding of school policy and school law
- Provide parents with calendars, notices, or other information that does not generally contain related information to the student.
- Your personal advocate
- Participation in school meetings
- Attend Truancy Court
- Attend Admission Review and Dismissal Meeting (ARD)
- One -on- One Support Service
- Due Process Hearings (DPH)
- Assist in the organization of your child's records
- Referrals and resources
- Educate on School Policy and School Law
- Easing the burden for "parents" on what to do and how to become more involved with their child's school

Parent-to-Parent Connection Advocacy, Inc.

Carolyn Ann Morris, *Parent Advocate*

ppca@sbcglobal.net

BIBLIOGRAPHY

Dietzman, A. (2023). 5 Ways to Help K–12 Students Advocate for Themselves—Tutor.com *A Service of The Princeton Review.*

IDEA. (2023, October 17). Retrieved from Individuals with Disabilities Education Act:
https://sites.ed.gov/idea/

Lee, A. M. (2023, October 5). *The Difference Between IEPs and 504 Plans.* Retrieved from Understood:
https://www.understood.org/en/articles/the-difference-between-ieps-and-504-plans

Lowry, K. K. (October 2023 17). Retrieved from ADD Advocate:
https://addadvocate.com/2016/12/02/iep-provide-free-appropriate-public-education-fape/

NOTES

NOTES

NOTES

NOTES

NOTES

NOTES

NOTES

NOTES

NOTES

NOTES

~PPCA~

PARENT TO PARENT CONNECTION ADVOCACY

ADVOCACY FOR ALL!

Est. 1989

Made in the USA
Columbia, SC
04 January 2024

29851514R00078